DIGITAL MONEY

THE SMART BUSINESS LEADER'S GUIDE TO STOPPING THE HACKER

DAVID STELZL

TABLE OF CONTENTS

Welcome to The Digital Megatrend

The Digital Megatrend, as some have called it, has the potential to turbocharge your business and change your life. Greater access, customer experience, and geographical reach are here. But disregard security and you may be out of business before you know it.

The Megatrend is Here, But What About Security?

This morning I'm sitting in Starbucks drinking a latte. I ordered it just minutes before arriving, using my Starbucks app. It's morning, time to wake up and get going after a night of "deep sleep" using my Brainwave app (which sets the brainwaves in order for restful sleep after a long day).

No physical money was exchanged. I paid using my app, showed up a few minutes later, and there it was, perfect and ready to drink. Welcome to the Digitalization Megatrend, where customer experience is paramount, and connecting is everything.

I use my phone to pay for groceries with Apple-Pay, order my drinks online, and even order pizza on Friday nights with an app. Last week I bought a coke from a vending machine with my phone, and in a few weeks, I'll be able to toss my debit card, in exchange for my phone app. I already deposit checks and transfer funds with my phone. If Amazon sold Starbucks, I would likely have stayed home and had it delivered by drone to my home office.

We're Going Digital – All the Way

When I started my business over a decade ago, my first meeting with my accountant was a wake-up call for him. He expected me to arrive at 10:00 AM. Instead, I called him. The phone is hardly part of the Digitalization Megatrend, but the fact that he expected me to drive across town in rush-hour traffic, to talk about business, was surprising to me. "I don't have time for that," I told him. I want to do everything online, and if necessary, we'll talk on the phone. Everything else is digital.

My banker was the same way. I had to stop in to open an account, but when my rep started showing me their beautiful lobby and work areas, I stopped her. "This is my last visit to your bank," I told her. "Show me your website. If I run into a problem, I may call support. But I don't plan on coming back. I bank by app, and use paperless reporting. If I run into trouble I may call support, but it will be after hours. There's no need to drive all the way down here again."

Last Christmas, and for several years now, Christmas shopping has been fun! Why? Because my wife and I collect ideas from our seven kids, head up to the mountains for the weekend, and camp out in a cabin, complete with high-speed Internet. Most of our shopping is done online with Amazon Prime free 2 day shipping. Why would anyone do it any other way?

This is the Digitalization Megatrend . Everything is connected, or will be. It changes everything…including security.

The Digitalized Megatrend – One of Your Biggest Opportunities – Also Your Biggest Threat

Your business is going digital. And it's happening fast. Obviously we all use computers and smartphones. That's not what I mean. I'm talking about a Megatrend. A complete paradigm shift in the way we think about business.

Think cloud, app store, smartphones, and Internet of Things (IoT). Everything is connected; everything is digital. This is the mindset of Generation C – C stands for connected, and they will be connected.

In just a couple of years, your business will be fully meshed with a generation of digitalized workers and leaders. Their world is online, including friends, family, photos, and entertainment. They bank on tablets, invest electronically, buy and sell on their smartphones, and transact business anywhere at any time. These people share their lives on Facebook, opt for a text message over a phone call, and hangout together in chat rooms rather than coffee shops.

This trend is unstoppable. To compete in the future, your company must be connected too. It must be mobile. It must be global. All of this is now possible, whether you're a Fortune 500 or a micro business operating in a spare bedroom.

This digital movement relies on what's been termed,

transformational technologies. The cloud, big data, online collaboration, social business, etc. With these space-age advancements, your business or start-up has an incredible opportunity. You have global reach. You can compete with Fortune 500 companies around the world. You can utilize enterprise class technology, simply by plugging in like a utility. All of this was out of reach just a decade ago.

If you work for a larger business, half of your applications are probably in a cloud somewhere. Your suppliers are connected, as are your customers. And social media has replaced in-person collaboration.

But What About Security?

But suddenly there's a need to reconsider security. We've already seen evidence of the disaster that awaits us if we don't wake up. Everything is online. Everything is accessible. Keeping it in the right hands will be overwhelmingly difficult. Over the past five years we've seen power grids disrupted, military secrets compromised, major retailers sifted of their customer's data, and some of the most intimate parts of our lives digitally exposed. And it will get worse.

So while your company must be digital, can your company handle these new threats? Threats that may surreptitiously take your most prized intellectual property (IP), and steal the trust of your most loyal customers.

What Happens to Your Data Security When Everything is Connected?

The security equation has changed. Twenty years ago we thought math would solve this problem. Encryption algorithms and authentication keys were the answer. We all realize now that keeping thieves out is more difficult than we originally thought. And with digitalization, you can expect the problem to get worse.

Who is Behind the Latest Cybercrime Disasters? Three Key Actors

There are three, primary "actors" in the hacker world; Traditional Cybercriminals, Hacktivists, and Spies (think espionage). In addition, significant threats may exist internally among the team members sitting nearby, as well as with contractors and third-parties you deal with.

Over the past decade, the emphasis has been on credit card theft and skimming money. But more recent attacks focus on much more. This is what Mike McConnell, former director of national intelligence, secretary of homeland security, and deputy secretary of defense, means when he writes, "The Chinese government has a national policy of economic espionage...in fact, the Chinese are the world's most active and persistent practitioners of cyber espionage today," He is accusing China of carrying out nation-state sponsored attacks. In reality, these are well-funded acts of war.

Recent U.S. security advisor reports add Russian hacker groups to this problem. Russian groups are thought to be far more sophisticated than the Chinese, and therefore, pose an even greater threat. Evidence suggests they are actively stealing U.S. innovations right now. My NSA contacts tell me these countries are working together behind the scenes because both need data from the U.S. to boost their individual economies. Many have called these acts of war, "The greatest transfer of wealth in history."

And, one more we'll mention, is the growing proliferation of social media and recruitment strategies coming from the group we refer to as ISIS, the radical Islamic movement that is less interested in stealing intellectual capital, and more interested in destruction.

Closer to Home: How is Cybercrime Impacting the Businesses Around You?

Obviously there is the financial loss. But these crimes also cut into jobs, your competitive advantage, and even national security. McConnell comments on how large-scale this problem is, stating, "We think it is safe to say that *large* easily means billions of dollars and millions of jobs."

The Internet is the ideal medium for stealing intellectual capital, money, and power. Hackers can easily penetrate systems that transfer large sums of data, while corporations and governments have a hard time identifying the specific perpetrators. As a result, this is seemingly impossible to stop, and few are brought to justice.

In a recent study, the 9/11 Security Commission reported back stating, "Our most pressing problems are the daily cyberattacks against the nation's most sensitive public and private networks." They later added, "Yet, because this war lacks attention-grabbing explosions and body bags, the American people remain largely unaware of the dangers." In the case of 9/11, we didn't awaken to the gravity of this terrorist threat until it was too late. Let's not repeat this mistake in the cyber-realm.

What Are Cybercriminals Really After?

As just mentioned, company secrets and intellectual property are the newest hacker targets. So who is at risk? The truth is, no business or individual is safe. But small businesses and entrepreneurial startups are often the primary targets for these perpetrators.

A recent WSJ headline reads, "Hackers target startups that secure early-stage funding." Startup companies are now detecting cyberattacks just after they raise their Series "A" funding. They're watching to see when funding is made available, knowing that there will be a sudden influx of cash. Another target is new innovation; your inventions. These groups are looking to advance without the R&D cost. To further exasperate this problem, recent patent law changes actually encourage the theft of intellectual property. The person who files first has an advantage over the patent right. That means that as you are inventing, others are watching. Suddenly, credit card theft is of little consequence compared to your ten-year R&D effort. A copycat product overseas might be enough to put your company out of business.

How Will a Digitalized World Worsen This Problem?

When it's digital, it's connected, and that means it's accessible. It doesn't matter if something has a password on it. It doesn't even matter if it's encrypted. Firewalls are no match for today's cybergangs. But as we necessarily move more toward the use of transformational technologies and IoT, we expose ourselves more and more.

Over the past decade you've probably secured your data behind network perimeters. Using firewalls, passwords, and encryption, you've felt fairly secure. However, there's an underlying flaw in this approach. I'll explain why in this book. The fact is, security starts with you. It involves anyone creating, using, or transmitting data.

Your move to transformational technology is necessary. But that necessarily means moving away from traditional perimeter security. Digitalization means connectivity, mobility, and an open computing architecture. If you're going to compete, all of this is necessary. As I've already stated, this is a great opportunity for the small business leader and the entrepreneur, as well as just about any business where leadership understands how to harness the power of connectivity and transformational technology.

But with it comes exposure. You can't control your data in someone else's cloud, and you don't oversee the network your employees are using at Starbucks. Your systems will, by design, face the public web, and your company no longer has any definable perimeter security. In the new world, your data is everywhere and accessible by just about anyone. And so, security must change.

What You Need to Know to Keep Your Data Safe

What's the one thing every office worker and business leader must understand? I call it The Impact vs. Likelihood Graph. Every business leader owns digital assets, and every knowledge worker uses them. Some of these assets are worth everything to your company. Others, not so much.

The Impact vs. Likelihood Graph explains how to view and assess data and risk, and how to make decisions regarding your use, what you expose, and how you safeguard the data you rely on for business today. In the following chapters, I will begin with an overview of what this is, and how you can start evaluating your own risk as you create and use data in your personal and professional life.

The value of data is changing rapidly and must be understood. Cybercurrencies and digital money are also a growing trend. Both may be considered as money. Not only data that represents money, but data that is worth money. I will be addressing both, as hackers are after both. Any data you possess, that can be turned into a profit on the black market, is at risk.

But security is, in many ways, more of a people problem than it is a technical one. The losses you read about everyday could have been prevented if people better understood how security works, and how data is compromised.

Getting the Most Out of This Book

In Part I of this book, I will be exploring some of the biggest trends in security and how you might be unknowingly exposing your personal and corporate assets to surreptitious attackers.

In Part II, I will show you the one big problem most companies are making with security. In fact, this isn't just a technical problem, it's a misunderstanding. As you'll see, this same mistake is starting to carry over in the physical security world. You will see it in some of our national security policies, as well as at the state level. In fact, some of the tragic news reports involving church and school mass shootings might have been prevented or minimized if this one principle had been understood by government officials and local bystanders. Fix this one thing, and 80% of your problem goes away.

Finally, in Part III, I present seven important mindsets, central to building awareness and a corporate culture that is security aware. The fact is, senior managers are a key part of making your business secure. Leave it to IT only, and you'll likely fail. IT can help select technology and put controls in place to enforce policy, but managers and knowledge workers must understand what makes data secure, how it is exposed, and how criminals are using *social engineering* tactics to talk you out of your most prized possessions.

Part One

WE'RE AT WAR

BUT BECAUSE WE DON'T SEE BODY BAGS COMING BACK FROM OVERSEAS, NO ONE SEEMS TO BE PAYING ATTENTION!

CHAPTER ONE

We're Losing

We're losing this battle simply because the people creating and using data in your office don't understand the enemy, the weapons, the motivations, and the mistakes every one of us are making as we enter a digitalized world.

Your company relies on data to make money. Call centers, designs, strategy, communication, it's all digital. Chances are you personally bank online. Have you ever considered what would happen if one day you logged into your bank account, only to find that the bank website had no record of your account? What would you do?

The truth is, we've built our lives on digital information. Our banking, mortgage, bill paying, and healthcare are all digital. How easy is it for a company to lose their data? Or to lose your account information? Can you prove that you had a certain sum of money in the bank, with concrete evidence that would demand they repay you? Few of us could. But take your money home and put it in your mattress, and suddenly you can't even function in this country.

Today, without bank accounts and credit cards, you can't rent cars, buy homes, reserve a hotel room, or pay for anything online. If you had to keep all of your records in physical formats, you'd probably have to rent a storage facility to keep the paperwork. And if your children have school work, it likely requires you to set up accounts online to access research tools and perhaps submit assignments. We live in a digital world, and there's no turning back.

Some have suggested that an EMP bomb could take out our electronics for a prolonged period of time. I'm not stocking up on food. But it could happen. Using the impact vs. likelihood graph, it's up to each individual to evaluate their risk levels, making choices as to where to increase security and resilience.

The good news is, a lot of the theft and disruption can be stopped or at least slowed, if computer users like you can better understand what's happening, how it's happening, and who is behind it. With a few basic security principles, and some change in mindset, you can start to build a culture of security both at home and in your business. One that will send criminals to the business next door where the leadership has failed to take the steps provided in this book.

Like the home invasions, if your home looks well protected, the burglars will continue down the street.

In just a few pages I will show you what's happening, and how to start protecting yourself from major losses both at home and at work. And it won't cost you a fortune, or require you to become a technical security geek. Apply a few simple principles and start thinking about security in a new way, and your life will be greatly simplified as you enter the Digitalized Megatrend World.

Understanding the War

This is the war no one sees. The war on drugs is evident. People of all ages are selling heroin, meth, and more deadly versions of these drugs such as krocodil that are taking users down a road they can't return from. While the dealers are not always easy to catch, law enforcement knows who they are. It's just a matter of time before they are caught. The problem is, arrests are slow, and proliferation is fast. We'll never win this war, but at least we know where it is, and how to avoid it.

The war on terrorism is harder. In this case, we are often far behind the planning. Government intelligence is pretty good at picking up communications and heading off terrorist attacks, but as we saw on 9/11 and with many more recent bombings and mass shootings, it's hard to tell one person from the next until it's too late. Technology often aids these groups in secret communication and planning, but this is not a cybercrime issue. It's a military operation using physical guns and explosives in most cases.

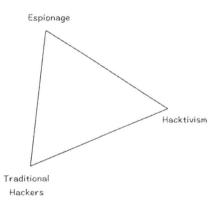

Data security is a different kind of issue. Attackers can be anywhere, and from all walks of life. As mentioned in the preface, these criminals come in three basic flavors: nation-state sponsored espionage attackers, hacktivists, and cybercriminals. All three are after your data, but all three have very different motives and sources of funding. The good news is, they are all using similar tools and methods, meaning, if we can figure out how they are attacking, we can start to take action.

Understanding the Big Attacks

If you're in small business, you might be thinking, "No one wants my data." That's not the case, but it is important to look at the larger attacks first to understand the power and funding behind these events.

Cyberattacks against your nation are happening daily. It doesn't really matter where you live. Foreign governments are watching each other. I live in the US. Our government has already stated that foreign governments are in our systems, trying to access data they should not have access to, on a daily basis. Our government officials have stated, "We know they are in, and the best we can do is work to keep them away from the extremely sensitive data."

Over the past few years we've seen plans for our President's helicopter taken, along with classified data regarding our fighter jet plans, and global surveillance technology. This data is showing up in different, and unexpected places. One Wall Street Journal writer posed the question, "Why does China's new fighter jet look so much like ours?" Nothing conclusive here, but in just about every major breach, either China or Russia seem to be on the list of the accused. Unfortunately, it's very difficult to prove anything. For instance, the Sony Pictures hack was blamed on North Korea, but without any proof, no one can really do anything about it.

And even if they could, how would that help Sony Pictures? The damage has been done, and no amount of blame or retaliation will recover their losses.

The big attacks tend to fall in line with the three actors

referenced above. In many of the reports, we see government data being taken (intelligence,) by nations we suspect, most likely in an attempt to keep tabs on what we are doing. In other cases, these same actors are likely stealing intellectual property to develop their own products for resale in a copycat market. When there's not R&D cost, the margins are much higher, making this kind of theft attractive.

When talking about a communist government, it makes sense that they would view intellectual capital as government property, whereas in the US, investors and shareholders see intellectual capital as their own competitive advantage. Data that should not be disclosed. The Office of Personnel Management (OPM) might fall into this category as it exposes the activities of US undercover agents operating around the world.

Other large scale hacking is taking place in the financial and retail space, stealing large amounts of data that can then be sold on the black market. Companies like Target, Home Depot, and JP Morgan fall into this category, each having exposed tens of millions of credit card and account numbers. The term "stolen" doesn't really work here since the stores still have the numbers. But they've been exposed and used on the black market, costing banks and customers a fortune. (Even if you don't think you are paying for credit card replacements, you are. The bank will make it up in fees.)

Finally, Sony Pictures might be categorized as a hacktivist attack based on suspicions that someone did not like the movie dealing with Kim Jong-Un. Other instances, not related to government, include attacks on companies like PayPal for expressing or supporting certain social views. News reports from the years 2013 – 2014 were filled with such attacks, mostly carried out by a group that calls themselves Anonymous.

The big lesson you should take away from these attacks, regardless of your company's size of vertical industry, is that these companies have spent millions on securing data, especially those in the financial sector. Retail companies like Home Depot and Target were deemed to be PCI (Payment Card Industry) compliant, meaning they had met the government's compliance laws. Yet, they were still defeated by cybercriminals.

One telling incident involved Hannaford, a grocery chain in New England. They were PCI compliant until breached. Once the breach was reported, their PCI compliance was revoked. In other words, those certifying PCI compliance assumed that PCI compliance should stop a breach. This is a wrong mindset; one I will address in Part III of this book.

Attacks Closer to Home

While the news is full of reports on very large companies, your small business and personal life are at risk as well. Small business has historically been the victim of data theft and ransomware. Ransomware, a software technology that sneaks into businesses through email attachments, infected websites, and downloaded programs, is taking our nation by storm. Doubling every year, over the past 3 or 4 years, companies reportedly paid out about 24 million dollars in ransom fees in 2015 just to get their data back. I will address some specific technologies you should be aware of in the upcoming chapters of Part I, but for now, the point is, both large and small businesses offer hackers an opportunity to make money with your data. Where there's money to be made, you can expect there to be attacks.

As everything around us becomes part of this globally connected world, The Digitalized Megatrend is opening up new avenues for hackers.

Small business is often the incubator for innovation and discovery. Serial entrepreneurs leave the large businesses to start these small businesses with an idea. Investors pour millions into these innovations, and new products emerge. Like Apple emerging from a small garage-based startup, or Dell from Michael Dell's college dorm room, new innovation is the heart-beat of the American economy, and there are people out there who would like to get their hands on it, once the hard work is done.

There are also the small time hackers, not capable of launching sophisticated attacks against a global bank, but who can profit quickly from ill-protected, smaller businesses, reselling stolen data or talking you and your team members into allowing them to transfer money right to an offshore account.

Over the past few years, we've seen demonstrations of hackers gaining access to ATM machines, elevators, cars, and even pacemakers. If it's computerized, it can likely be hacked. And once hacked, there's probably a way to make money from it. Most of your work is connected right now, and chances are, people are already looking into your data, your systems, and your life, trying to find an angle to profit from it.

We Are at War

This is a war. It's a kind of cyberwar. And we are losing the battle every day, mostly because of a pervasive unawareness about what is possible, and what can be used to make money.

Because there are no body bags coming back from overseas, few are paying attention to the threat at hand. Instead, we continue to build our world on digital platforms without regard for protection. Read through Dietrich Bonhoeffer's life story and you will get a sense of how Hitler and his Nazi Reich crept into power with public support, only to become one of the most devastating events in history.

In the same way, we are letting the government impose expensive compliance laws on business, without really understanding the threat or how to stop it. Continue, and soon your entire world will be online, easily taken and misused for someone else's profit. While you might not be tortured, it is possible to lose everything, including a small business you might own.

Over fifteen years ago, my longtime friend John Sileo, author of *Privacy Means Profit*, lost just about everything but his family after carelessly tossing a piece of paper in the trash. That paper contained just enough information for someone to steal his identity and strip him of just about everything he owned. As he tells his story, he lost everything: his business, his money, and his name.

John was strong enough to rebuild. But the lesson was learned. In fact, John went on to rebuild an entire business around helping others secure their data. Today, he is traveling the world sharing his story, and showing people how to take charge of their digital assets. My hope is that you'll read this book to gain a better understanding of the war you are in. And from it, you will begin taking steps of action to secure both your personal and professional life. If we all start doing this, we can create a more stable future for our children. It is my hope and prayer that we'll all do this, so that all of our children can enjoy the freedom and economic growth I've experienced in my time on this planet.

The Price of Inaction

The alternative is unknown. It might be cyberwar, or it might be identity theft. Large scale destruction is possible through software and networks. We've seen this firsthand in the destruction on Iran's uranium enrichment program. It might be smaller scale identity theft, such as what John Sileo experienced. Smaller scale, yet extremely damaging to that individual.

Either way, more connectivity means greater risk. Can you imagine a way to continue if your bank account is gone, or if credit card fees double? Will you feel protected by your government if your compliance regulations become so expensive that small business owners (the largest producer of jobs in the US) can no longer afford to keep their businesses?

As you've seen in this first section, the weapons of this war are powerful. They break into governments, major corporations, and scale down to the smallest business or individual. They are capable of picking out one computer around the globe, and taking it out, or sending out small attacks across millions of computers at the press of a button. This is a war we can't stop with brute force. It's going to take some rethinking, and the development of some new habits. It all starts with you and some minor adjustments to how you work and think about data security, and your online digital world.

CHAPTER TWO

Digital Money and Data Value

Some of your data is worth money. Some of it is money. As you'll see, it doesn't really matter how you define it, the growing value of data makes all data values grow, and the same security issues apply to both intellectual capital and cybercurrencies .

Digital Money. When I say digital money, I mean both data that represents money, and data that commands a high price on the market, what we might call the Darknet, or those chat rooms you sometimes see on television. So before we launch into a discussion on what is happening in the data world, it is important to lay some foundation as to what is happening in the digital world of data and cybercurrencies first.

Cybercurrencies and Real Money

Bitcoin is a cybercurrency, but certainly not the only one out there.

There are hundreds of these online forms of money. What is a cybercurrency? Simply a new form of money that only exists in the digital world. It's not governed by a nation and not overseen by the Federal Reserve or any other government agency.

One misconception is that Bitcoin is bad, or only used by hackers. This is not the case. Hackers use it because it's anonymous. Unlike PayPal, which is just a computerized way of paying with your bank account or credit card, a cybercurrency can be, but is not always anonymous. There is no central authority.

In general, the cybercurrency is virtual, encrypted, and uses an online ledger or blockchain. A blockchain is simply the online ledger. In the case of Bitcoin, it's anonymous and accessible by anyone with a Bitcoin account. In other cases, that ledger may be private, meaning the cybercurrency can only be used by an internal group of users.

Different cybercurrencies are created with different advantages, depending on what that currency will be used for. In the case of Bitcoin, the paying person is anonymous. In another virtual currency, GreenCoinX, the user is not. But in both cases, the currency is designed to be fast, easy to use, and independent of government oversight. And since there is no central authority, there is no middleman. So there are no bank processing fees! If you take credit cards in your business, no-fee cybercurrencies may suddenly be appealing. Note, there is also no PCI compliance to deal with!

Some currencies work for hackers because they are anonymous. Others are built to replace cash where people tend to be in a cash society, but are doing more on their phone as we go digital. Currencies like Bitcoin are also used by people selling things that would be considered illegal. This could mean anything from child pornography to drugs. Still others are designed to pay people online. Dogecoin would be an example.

Cybercurrency adoption has been slow, probably because

people seem to trust the bank more than they do an online ledger controlled by a group outside any branch of government. However, a cybercurrency such as Bitcoin is, in a sense, just another account like your bank account.

Your Bank Account is Online and Digital

The interesting thing is, your bank account is also digital, just like Bitcoin. Your bank doesn't have your money. Your money is just a bunch of data on a digital ledger. But in this case, it's controlled by a central authority and valued like the U.S. Dollar.

If you use FDIC insured accounts, you feel some level of comfort in believing that your money is protected when you make a deposit. But the truth is, there are limits on FDIC protection. Many of your investment accounts are not covered, and if you have a small business checking account, you might find you have very little standing between it and the hacker. If someone starts transferring money out of your account, you will find that the bank does not treat it like a personal, direct deposit account. I have never tried to collect on FDIC insurance, but I understand that getting your money back may be much harder than you think.

What would you do if you opened up your browser later today, only to discover that your bank balance was now zero, overdrawn, or completely gone? Would you call the bank and expect them to believe you?

You trust your bank. But your money is all digital, and this should cause you some concern. This data is likely some of the most important data you own, but its protection is largely out of your hands.

Data and Data Aggregation

Early hacking efforts have focused on banks and credit cards. Visa and MasterCard have had standards like the current PCI standards in place for years to provide some level of protection over your card.

But credit cards and banks are not the only datasets worth money. As businesses collect more and more data, and move more data to the cloud, hackers are finding more ways to take it and make money with it.

Later in this book, I will be addressing the power of data aggregation, and how your data grows in value as it is aggregated with other data. For example, it may not matter to you if someone knows you bought a new pair of pants today at the store. However, when computers start putting all of your data together, they start figuring out things that you didn't want to pass on. That might include medical issues, legal affairs, or some dark secret you really didn't want to share.

Even those with nothing to hide (which is really no one), have data worth money. The power of computers to figure out how you think, and how to move you to buy, is far more impressive than you might imagine. You might think you won't give into advertisements targeting you after you search for something online, but the truth is, advertising works, and companies are getting extremely proficient at talking us into buying stuff we don't need. Carry that out to how you vote, religious convictions, and even prejudices you didn't think you had, and suddenly you're no longer thinking for yourself.

If you think you're above this type of manipulation, read some books on the science of marketing and influencing people's decisions, and you'll see that it's true.

Some of the data you should care about includes your personal information, intellectual capital, financial data, and customer data. But it also often includes the things you share on social media, in a supposedly secure group.

Personal Data

In the coming chapters, I address trends in the hacker world. One of those trends focuses in on social media. Over the past decade we have all been talked into exposing more and more of our personal lives online.

Today's hackers can learn a lot just by sifting through social media data. This then leads to pretexting, pretending to be someone who knows us, with the intent to deceive us. It's one thing to use social media to market your business. But my advice is to stop posting your life on Facebook.

Facebook is using you to make millions on your data. Facebook advertising knows just about everything there is to know about you, your income, your hobbies, your belief system, and more. If you've never set up a Facebook ad, it might be worth going through the motions just to see what I'm talking about. And it doesn't matter what you've posted, today's computers can predict all kinds of things about you with amazing accuracy.

In addition, your personal data can be used to buy things you'll never see, put you into debt in ways you won't believe, and allow someone else to become you, just long enough to take a loan in your name. If you think your electronic medical records are safe online, you're mistaken.

Intellectual Capital

Your intellectual capital is worth a fortune to those overseas. If you live in the U.S. and own a small business, or work for a high-tech medical firm, people want your data.

Innovation is lacking in many parts of the world, and as countries struggle to build their economies, your innovations might offer a solution. Anything that looks like an invention, process improvement, or secret formula, is a target. Nation-states want it, and they'll do almost anything to get it.

Financial Data

Financial data has always been a target. Today, hackers are coming up with all kinds of ideas on how to get people in your company to send them money. Ransomware is just one example. Millions of dollars are being paid out every year by people who need their data back.

Your accounting information, employee payroll, and customer payment information is all at risk. Every day we read about credit cards being taken, wire transfers that should never have happened, and people's banking credentials being stolen.

Customer Data

Finally, your customer data is worth money. Competition is growing, especially as the Digitalization Megatrend takes our businesses to a global level. Your customer lists, their payment information, and any data you might hold that hackers can resell for money is all at risk.

When a small business reports a hack, there's a 50% chance they'll go out of business in the next year. Larger companies like

Home Depot and Target, who have lost large amounts of customer data, have experienced major dips in share prices, as well as declines in customer satisfaction. Your customers expect you to take care of their data, especially when it's sensitive data that could cause them to lose their job, status, or disrupt their personal life.

Deep Machine Learning, Big Data Analytics, and the Growing Value of Data

The Digitalization Megatrend introduces enormous opportunities, but with it comes a whole new level of risk. Deep machine learning refers to computers that use artificial intelligence to predict and profile things far beyond what people are doing.

Data aggregation means the compiling of large amounts of data, which can then be analyzed to figure out all kinds of things about a person. In the hands of the wrong person, these systems can do major damage.

From manipulation to pretexting, a person or company can be quickly stripped of their money, integrity, reputation, and their entire business. The next step is to rethink security.

CHAPTER THREE

The One Thing You Need to know

Without a clear understanding of your enemy, your assets, and the likelihood of attack, you can't really know what to invest in, how to protect yourself, or even if you've already been hit.

Several years and thirty pounds ago, I was enjoying the Christmas holiday season with my family and some out of town friends here in Charlotte, NC. I was probably enjoying this season too much. In fact, I had been eating junk food since Thanksgiving! Generally our family is pretty health conscious, but this one year, I was taken with my oldest son's love for baking, and eating everything in sight. By the time Christmas day came, it was catching up with me.

By mid-afternoon, I was not feeling well. With our company and the kids entertaining each other, I managed to make it through the afternoon and evening, but I was really looking forward to lying down for the night. But when bedtime finally arrived, I found myself tossing and turning, unable to sleep. Something was definitely wrong.

Around 4 AM, my wife was deep into a dream, but I was done, ready to get up. I needed some advice. So I headed down the hall to consult my health advisor; Google (Actually, my wife is my health advisor).

It's another sign of the Digitization Megatrend. Don't most of us go to Google first when we need information?

After about 30 minutes of searching, I had stumbled upon several sites talking about early heart attack symptoms. My father had his first heart attack around age 40, so I knew it was in the family history. And I was now worried that it might be happening to me. I didn't really want to share this with my family until I was sure. The site I had found listed 10 major telltale signs to look for. As I went down the list, each one seemed to confirm my suspicion. It was frightening, but I knew I had to tell someone.

Before I could even finish, my wife suspected the heart problem. Being a retired health professional, she immediately hurried me out to the car, calling back to the kids to pack some things for the hospital. I could see this was going to be a big ordeal.

Once at the ER, the tests began. They were checking for signs of a recent heart attack, as well as indications of a pending attack. As the morning progressed, the test results started to trickle in. The good news? I had not had a heart attack, nor was I about to have one, as far as they could tell. My cholesterol was high, as were my triglycerides, but there was no immediate indication of a blockage. Still, they did want to run a stress test and keep me overnight for observation.

Here's where things got interesting.

It turned out that the facility, which I had never been to, did not actually have hospital beds. It's just a very large ER facility. The nurse came by to let me know that they would be transporting me across town to the larger hospital where I would have a bed.

It was at that moment that it occurred to my wife to check on our insurance policy to see whether or not they would cover this transport. Up until now, money had not been a concern. We were working on a life threatening event, and that's all that mattered. But now, with no immediate threat, we wanted to know.

My wife came back shortly after calling our insurance company. "They won't cover a non-emergency transport." After some discussion, I learned that they would charge us about $1500 to take this 15 minute ride across town. Wow!

I was not about to pay $1500 for a 15 minute car ride. No matter how luxurious the ambulance might be, I wasn't giving in on this. But when I tried to get the nurse to see my point of view, she just shook her head and walked out. Moments later the doctor came in, clip board in hand, and simply said, "Mr. Stelzl, you have to take the ambulance. You're under our care, and we are responsible for your health. They'll be here in five minutes."

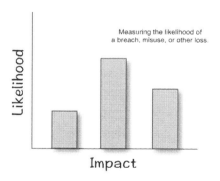

I could tell she was pretty firm on this, but I continued to argue that I was not willing to pay the $1500. She continued on about my heart, my cholesterol, and what my family would do if I were to die today. I could see I wasn't getting anywhere. It was time to pull out the Impact vs. Likelihood Chart.

The One Thing You Need to Know Before You Can Make a Wise Decision About Data Security

The Impact vs. Likelihood Chart is a simple tool I use to measure risk. It's a simple X vs. Y axis from my Algebra-I days. The X-axis represents a measurement of impact based on your most important digital assets.

If you were looking at personal data, my guess is your banking or investment assets would be pretty far to the right on the axis. If you use online investing tools, not only do you want to make sure your data is accurate, you also want immediate access to these assets. If the market starts heading down, you might want to sell. If your site is unavailable, you'll be upset! If your bank balance is wrong, that's also going to be a major problem. And if you have some sort of health condition that you don't want exposed, having your online EMR (electronic medical record) data compromised will leave you extremely upset.

As a small business owner, an unauthorized wire transfer that your banker refuses to cover could put you out of business. A breach of your clients' personal data could do the same. In larger organizations like OPM (The U.S. Office of Personnel Management, Hacked in 2015) and Target (Hacked in 2015), CIOs with high profile careers and big paychecks lost everything. Their reputations were tarnished in the press, and who knows if they will ever recover.

My doctor was highlighting these impact issues for me. She was pointing out my life assets: my heart, my family, my quality of life, and letting me know that there would be a tremendous impact if these things were mishandled. But I wasn't buying it. Why?

The Impact vs. Likelihood has just as much to do with likelihood as it does impact. I can scare you with high impact issues all day long. Some people will be moved, others won't. It's common for people to focus on impact when pushing you to do something. But few have an accurate way to show likelihood.

Messages like, "Buy gold now before the economy collapses," "Build a bomb shelter before Y2000 hits," or whatever the next big scare is, push people to do something. Many of us have been burned by this and will refuse to move on future calls to action. And rightly so; we deserve to hear about the likelihood. In fact, we need to hear about likelihood.

It's true that a nuclear bomb could be launched right now, targeting my office. But what is the likelihood? If it's high, it's time to run (Of course that won't do much to change the outcome). My house could burn down, my kids could get into an accident, and I could become so frightened that I refuse to go outside or let my kids do anything fun. But I would be living in a prison built in my own mind.

When I start looking at likelihood, things begin to come into perspective. My neighborhood is fairly safe. I live out in the country, and it's highly unlikely that a car will hit my kids playing in the front yard. We are not at war, at least not a physical war, on US soil, so I feel pretty certain that we won't see a nuclear bomb today. We might have an act of terrorism, but probably not in my home town. At least we never have had one.

When I brought this chart out at the hospital, it was clear. They understood. Of course, I didn't really show them a physical chart, but in the case of data security, you actually do need a graph.

I was afraid. In my mind, the likelihood had been high when my wife drove me to the ER. I was willing to submit myself to all kinds of testing, without asking questions. I didn't let money get in the way of me being with my family or living the rest of my life. But now, with the results coming back clear, I was feeling better. When I explained this to the doctor, her argument no longer made sense. My likelihood was no greater today than it was yesterday. And yesterday, I hadn't even gone to the doctor. At that point, she gave up, gave me a pile of discharge papers to sign, and I was free to go. My wife drove me to the hospital, we checked in as a new patient, and started the next phase of investigation.

That next morning I was released with a good stress test result, and some instructions to get my cholesterol down. There was no immediate threat. Since that day, I've lost weight, lowered my cholesterol, and started a daily exercise routine along with better eating habits.

If you don't know what your likelihood is, it will be hard to make wise decisions about how to better secure your data.

Here's What Your Board of Directors Really Wants to Know

If your company has a board, they probably meet quarterly. Here's what they really want to know about data security.

- ☐ What are the top three to five threats?

- ☐ What are the odds the company will encounter some kind of hack or major outage over the next twelve months?

- ☐ How are we trending? Are we getting better or worse?

- ☐ How are we managing security and risk; how are we keeping up with potential threats?

Your IT leadership team will have about twenty minutes to present your impact vs. likelihood graph in a two-day board meeting. If they are well prepared, they will know what the most important assets are, where they are, and what things could threaten them. Things that affect the three pillars of security:

- ☐ Confidentiality

- ☐ Integrity

- ☐ Availability

The problem is, building an impact vs. likelihood graph for a major corporation is not that easy. But that is the job of your CISO and their security team. In a smaller company, I recommend a third party provider that possesses this kind of experience.

On a personal level, it's important that you have some idea of what would create a threat in your digital world, and how to best guard against it. In the remaining pages of Part I, I will take you through seven major trends I see in cybersecurity, and what you should be doing to avoid being victimized.

As you'll see, many of them lead to wrong mindsets that are exposing data. In most cases, they all go back to three tools prevalent in most of the cybercrime reports you've seen in the news. They are bots, phishing scams, and social engineering. In most cases, one of two motivations are involved: terrorism or financial gain. The latter being the most likely of the two.

CHAPTER FOUR

Threat One: Software You Didn't Know Existed

Unauthorized software is likely installed on the computers your company uses – It has the power to steal your money, watch you work, and even pretend to be you.

Your computer hardware works because of the software on it. The operating system, the apps you download, and the applications that either run on your computer, or that are accessed through your Internet browser (cloud applications), drive your business. It all exists to create, use, transmit, and store data, the digital money we're interested in.

You can do a lot through software, and the growing trend is to replace hardware with more software (for example, software defined networks). Unfortunately, software is both good and bad. It's up to the software writers and users as to whether technology is used to benefit life or destroy it. And mistakes in software are what often open the door for those with evil intent.

In the hacker's case, software is usually used to make money more than to destroy. But then there are cases where destruction is at the heart of the attack, vandalism, or terrorism.

Either way, whether it's financial loss or physical destruction, it's important to know how software threats work, the current trends, and what you can do to reduce the likelihood of negative impact.

Understanding the Software Threat

My goal is to not get super technical here. Entire books have been written on malicious software and coding. I am assuming you understand what software is in general. The point here is to give you, the business leader, some insights on what hackers are doing to gain access to your data using software.

Hardware can be hacked, but most of the time, this means that the manufacturer (such as a maker of computer hardware), is tampering with the hardware to create "backdoors" into the computers they sell. In just about every case, this is more easily done with software. So let's assume the software is the problem area.

When a manufacturer puts a backdoor in their software, allowing others to gain access, it's bad news. This is what the FBI was asking Apple to do. It's hard to detect, and extremely hard to stop. No customer wants to hear that there's a backdoor in the product they've purchased. But it's also rarely reported or even suspected (although this is a growing concern).

On the other hand, software is easy to modify, easy to compromise, and extremely powerful. What am I talking about? Here's a list of possible malicious programs being used today:

☐ Viruses

☐ Worms

☐ Adware

☐ Botware and Botnets

☐ Ransomware

☐ Root Kits

☐ Spyware

These are the tools of the trade. Since this book is not written for the complete beginner, I assume you already have a working knowledge of these malware agents. If not, a simple Google search will give you the definitions you need.

The important things to understand here are the advancements being made, and the power behind the attacks you're hearing about. There was a time when people questioned just how much physical destruction was possible through a software program. But, while politicians have downplayed the destructive power of hackers, countries are at war using these very tools to destroy physical infrastructure such as power grids and dams.

Examples Close to Home: Software Attacks

Whether it's a bot, ransomware, a rootkit, or hidden backdoors purposely left in production software, software applications and operating systems are the predominant target for these malware weapons. So just how powerful is malware, and what can it really do?

Stuxnet: Physical Destruction and Much More

A few years ago, researchers in Germany detected something online that seemed to be targeting programming logic controllers (PLCs) used in manufacturing. It was a long and difficult study, but eventually they figured out that it was specifically targeting

Siemens equipment. However, these researchers were not observing anything destructive about this rogue software. After months of analysis, it was determined that this software was circulating around the Internet (globally) looking for a specific Siemens computer. In 2009 it landed.

The target was Iran. The malware was looking for Siemens computers used in the uranium enrichment process, perhaps the manufacturing of nuclear weapons. This particular stain of malware was dubbed StuxNet.

Meanwhile, Iranian workers were observing erratic behavior on the centrifuges used in their production process. They had Siemens engineers onsite trouble shooting, but with little success. Behind the scenes, this software was making the systems appear to operate normally, when in reality, it was spinning up the centrifuges to their resonant frequency. The vibrations apparently destroyed these systems, setting the Irian nuclear program back by about two years, according to news reports.

This is significant. One piece of software, roaming the earth, looking for one computer, and then, once found, installing itself on that system. Then, hiding itself from the engineers, while secretly destroying a physical manufacturing plant. This is the beginning of real-life cyberwarfare.

The First Power Grid Take Down: Ukraine

This attack was launched one afternoon against the Prykarpattyaoblenergo control center, which distributes power to Ukrainian residents. Malware was used to give an outsider access to the computer that controls circuit breakers at a nearby control station.

This was not a sudden attack. It took months of planning, including reconnaissance, the theft of an operator's credentials, and finally, the actual attack.

In this case, the operator was actually sitting at his desk, watching his cursor open the controls for the affected circuit breakers as the hacker took control and cut off power for a large

group of Ukrainian residents. Apparently, he tried to take back control, but was powerless as thousands of residents lost their lights and heat at the click of a mouse.

Locked out of his computer, the attacker managed to manually move 30 substations offline with direct access to their SCADA software. Over 230,000 residents lost power that day. Not only that, but he also cut the power at the station, leaving the operators to scramble for control in the dark.

The malware portion was used to take control, collect passwords, and then grant access to the person controlling the shutdown. So a combination of manual intervention and software stealing code allowed this attack to succeed.

In the aftermath, the damage was significant. Firmware was overwritten, systems were corrupted, and it took the Ukraine workers months to restore operations to their normal state.

Water and Dam Systems Run on Software Too

Perhaps this was payback for Stuxnet. The U.S. never claimed responsibility, along with its supposed partner, Israel. But Iran believes we did it.

In 2016, the US accused Iran of attacking New York dams and financial systems. Groups such as the Islamic Revolutionary Guard Corps have been accused of extensive cyber campaigns that targeted a dam outside New York City. In addition, several banks were hit by denial of service attacks, believed to be orchestrated by the same group.

In the case of the bank attacks, hackers were working to shut down online banking systems, making them unavailable to bank customers. These attacks reportedly ran the banks tens of millions of dollars in remediation costs.

The New York dam was attacked using the SCADA system, similar to the attack on the Ukraine. Bowman Avenue Dam, located in Rye, New York, is used to control flood waters. Done right, this type of attack could easily cause major floods, wiping out entire towns. The remediation efforts ran New York over $30,000.

These are calculated attacks, designed by sophisticated groups and governments, that have the potential to inflict major damage, cause death, and cost a lot of money. They are designed, not for profit, but to bring harm to American people. They are acts of terrorism, being carried out by software programs designed to destroy.

Other Major Business and Infrastructure Related Attacks

Other groups that have launched similar attacks include Unit 61398 of the Third Department of The Chinese People's Liberation Arm. Back in 2014, five Chinese military hackers were indicted for hacking, economic espionage, and other cybercriminal activity directed at Americans in the US. Their target? Nuclear power, metal production, and the solar products industries. Some of the companies affected include Westinghouse Electric, SolarWorld AG, United States Steel Corp, Allegany Technologies, Inc., and

Alcoa Inc.

Daily News reports tell us that China, Iran, Russia, and even North Korea are relentlessly attacking and probing our computer networks, looking for ways to conduct cyber espionage, and to disrupt and destroy critical infrastructure (including military, oil and gas, energy and utilities, transportation, hospitals, telecommunications, technology, education, aerospace, defense, chemical, and other government entities).

Everything we do relies on software at some level. These attacks speak to the power of software, and the vulnerable state many of us are in.

Using Software to Steal Money

If you look at just about any major cybercrime over the past year, software was used. The bot, that robotic code that gives hackers access to your computer, is central to most hacks you read about.

In most cases, this bot technology is used to take over computers, not for destruction, but to siphon off money or data with market value.

Do hackers care what that data is? Not really. In the past, hackers wanted actual money. The idea was to steal a small fraction of each transaction, or grab millions of credit cards. That still happens, and it's rampant. But your other data is worth money too. Sometimes the hacker doesn't even know what they'll do with the data, but they'll take it. Behind the scenes, teams will collaborate over data, looking for a way to make money with it. It might be fraud, selling to a competitor, or adding it to other aggregated data to give their existing database more worth.

Who's at Risk?

Software can do amazing things. It can launch a rocket,

manufacture something, or help you sleep at night. But as you can see, it can also do some incredibly damaging things. Software that was designed to attack comes in silently to steal, kill, and destroy. It's nearly impossible to stop, very hard to detect, and often overlooked as it carries out its mission.

Surreptitious Attacks Prey on the Uninformed

If you look around and don't see anything suspicious, it doesn't mean you're okay. In fact, when I hear IT personnel saying, "We've got this covered," I get concerned. Like the heart attack scare, once you see it, it's too late.

Who is at risk? Office workers who think IT has it covered, and executives who have delegated security to a generalist IT worker. Or the IT person who disregards the warnings coming from true security experts who possess the tradecraft.

People who do security part time will miss the subtle symptoms in the same way that a family doctor may miss signs that would be obvious to a seasoned cardiologist.

Your best defense is knowing how this software gets in, and avoiding some simple mistakes that give hackers easy access. With this in mind, let's look at a few common software problems that lead to major data breaches.

Digital Money Comes in Many Forms

Does your company have data that commands a high value on the Darknet?

> **Definition**: A **darknet** (or **dark net**) is "an overlay network that can only be accessed with specific software, configurations, or authorization, often using non-standard communications protocols and ports. Two typical darknet types are friend-to-friend networks (usually used for file sharing with a peer-to-peer connection), and privacy networks

such as Tor (software designed for anonymous Internet communication)."[1]

Chat rooms and eBay-like bidding sites exist throughout the darknet, providing a platform to buy and sell stolen digital goods.

Cybercurrencies such as Bitcoin are used to purchase anonymously, without oversight or the fear of getting caught. If your company creates, stores, or transmits financial data such as banking information, online criminals want it. If you have medical data that can be used to fraudulently acquire expensive medical equipment, that too is worth a lot on the black market.

Manufacturing processes, government secrets, secret formulas (like the recipe for Coke, or the rubber used in Michelin Tires)…it's all worth money, and someone is out there looking for an easy-to-open door to access it.

Does Your Company Have Mission Critical Systems? Extortion May be Your Next Hurdle

Ransomware is one of the fastest growing threats online today. Especially for small and medium businesses.

Ransomware bandits used to charge one bitcoin to unlock data (a ransom fee equivalent to about $400 USD). Times are changing as hackers learn. The faster companies pay, and the more they get away with it, the more they'll charge.

In 2015, Hollywood Hospital had their data encrypted, locking them out of patient data, treatment protocols, and everything they needed to keep their patients' healthcare on track.

Once encrypted, hackers demanded a $17,000 ransomware payoff to decrypt it. The FBI encourages companies not to pay the ransom. After all, if you pay it, the hackers are likely to come back with more demands, or be encouraged to move to more locations

---

[1] Wikipedia - Darknet

like yours. But what can a hospital full of sick and dying people do? They were forced to pay. The FBI has no way to bring justice to the hacker, and the time it would take to crack the encryption could put lives in danger. They paid.

This type of attack is doubling every year as hackers win against helpless victims. In fact, just after Hollywood, several other hospitals were hit with similar attacks. They all ended up paying. Then a month later, Calgary University paid a whopping $20,000 to regain access to their data.

Both small and medium businesses should be especially cautious here. Both tend to rely on IT administrators more than true security professionals, and given the cost of security, these businesses are often relying on the minimum to protect their data.

There are some simple things companies can do to greatly reduce the likelihood of getting hit with this type of attack, which I will be addressing later in this chapter.

The most interesting part of this growing crime is the customer service side. Hackers are actually setting up sites to help their victims walk through the payment process. I've read about customer service numbers one can call to get clarification on payments and negotiations, where victims have been able to negotiate a lower fee. It's almost as if the hacker is building a "service provider relationship" with their victim. One article talked about doing a trial decryption to demonstrate that the data would be restored after the fee was paid. It was a sort of "try and buy" offered by the hacker.

Is Your Software Up-to-Date? Or Are You Looking to Save Money?

Software is full of bugs; errors in the code. That's why you get software-update messages every week. It doesn't matter if it's a laptop, a phone, or your car. The problem is, we are used to updating software on the laptop. Routers, switches, phones, and cars may be neglected.

The industry average on errors runs between 10 and 50 errors per thousand lines of code. A simple Google search will confirm that. Most of the hacks used to take over your computer depend on some vulnerability or error found in the software.

Software companies, such as Microsoft, want to be known as "secure", but the competition often wins on features. Getting the code out early matters. In the case of phone software releases, this is especially true. There are about 50 million lines of code in Windows 10. So if you do that math, you can see there are a lot of bugs. Add your Office Suite, accounting software, and even virus protection, and we're talking about a lot of errors.

On the one hand, you want to apply security patches as they come out. At the same time, you can expect software updates to contain new bugs. Will they be more or less secure than the last one? Unknown. A patch can easily open up even bigger holes.

A recent Wall Street Journal article pointed out that Symantec's primary software engine that runs across twenty-five different Norton security products, is flawed and exposing millions of users to security risks. Can Symantec fix something this big fast enough? We'll have to wait and see. The writer recommends "upgrading" to another brand of anti-virus software. This can't be good news for Symantec.

What if that were true of your Microsoft Office software? Changing brands might not be that easy.

The key here is staying in tune with patches. Whoever oversees your security, should be on top of the latest security patches across all devices. And when something is EOL (end of life) it should be replaced. Your old software won't stop the new threats.

Wait, There's More

Yes, there's more. In the coming chapters I'll be addressing other specific areas that mostly relate to software in some form or another, but are created through wrong mindsets or specific applications of technology that may be pervasive in your business.

The problem with digital money is, it's all software. The programs you use to create data, the online accounting of your money, and even the software used to secure your money, it's all software with bugs. And it can all be exploited by the hacker. At this point, you should be asking, "Is there any hope?" There is, but it will take some work to get back to a secure state.

Steps You Can Take to Reduce Your Exposure

Most of the things I just mentioned are the responsibility of your IT department and/or the software developer. But there are some things you can do, at work and at home, to avoid becoming a victim of malware, bots, and ransomware.

- ☐ **Don't Open All Email**. It's hard to do, but don't open anything that looks like spam. No matter how enticing it is, email is not the place to receive advertisements and explore interesting links. Instead, Google things you might be interested in and look for sites that sell it. While a website can be compromised, email is much more likely to be your enemy.

- ☐ **Turn on Spam Filters**. Gmail and other popular mail programs provide them. Use them. These programs are pretty good at screening out advertisements, some of which will contain malware. The problem with spam is not clogged inboxes or unwanted pornography, even though both are aggravating. It's malware transmitted to your computer.

- ☐ **Delete Attachments That Don't Make Sense**. Never open Zip files attached to an email, unless the sender explicitly tells you they are sending it in a zip format. Also, Word documents that have extensions DOT, or anything other than the standard document extensions like *.docm, should not be opened. These file types contain macros that can execute malware on your computer.

☐ **Steer Clear of Sites Known for Malware**. Searching through pornographic sites, gambling sites, unfamiliar discount sites, and anything that says, "Peer to Peer" or P2P, can only lead to trouble. While there are legitimate sites for these things, the average person will not be able to discern the fake ones. A malware infection is suddenly highly likely.

☐ **Apply Software Updates**. This includes phone and computer. Software developers such as Microsoft and Apple constantly release updates when they discover malware designed to compromise the older versions. Most malware can be stopped simply by being up to date. Never run software that has been deemed EOL (end of life, meaning the developer is no longer supporting it or patching it.) At this point, the company no longer supports it, and no longer maintains its security.

If you look through news reports of hacks, you'll find that the majority of them do not use sophisticated hacking techniques. More often than not, if that company had been up to date on their patches or had the proper spam controls in place, they would not have been compromised.

While this is not always the case, it is a great first step toward keeping your money and data safe.

CHAPTER FIVE

Threat Two: Using Your Own Stuff

> BYOD is here: Bring Your Own Device. In a digitalized society BYOD is necessary. However, with it comes numerous mindset changes that are opening doors to criminals in ways you've never imaged.

Malware is a big deal, but mobility is creating a much bigger hole for malware to creep in. I'm not against BYOD (Bring Your Own Device), but some important mindset changes come with this trend that are greatly affecting your security and exposure.

With the explosive growth in smartphone technology, your end-users are going to use their own devices (phones, tablets, and even laptops). Millennials especially, live inside their phones and tablets. Even those of us who are part of the Baby Boomer generation are moving this way.

The phone, while not all that secure, is the future control center for just about everything we do. Banks are moving away from debit cards, and going to phone access. Hotels, restaurants, and event vending machines now allow customers to access their rooms, order their food, perform banking functions, and pay for goods and services, all through their phone. Life without a smart phone will be hard in the coming years. But ask me to carry two, and I won't.

I want my personal and professional life all in one place. Banking, music, movies, contacts, Evernote files, and access to company applications have to all be on one device. I carry both a laptop and smartphone, but don't ask me to keep switching back and forth. There are some scenarios that work well on the laptop such as writing this book. Checking email, buying a coke, or using an ATM has to be on my phone.

In the next few years, I expect employees to be insistent about this. Remember the mid 90s? Companies actually told us they would not be allowing their people to use the Internet unless the job required it. Imagine recruiting at your local university today and telling your prospective employees that you don't allow Internet access on the job. My guess is they'll pass on most opportunities with this criteria.

Understanding the Threat: I am My Own IT Department

In a recent report, Gartner Group predicted that "By 2020, one third of successful attacks experienced by enterprises will be on their shadow IT resources."[2]

Shadow IT means any IT service or product not supplied or endorsed by the IT organization. The reality is, your business is engaging with shadow IT resources even if you don't know it. Every time they download an app or set up a rogue access point, they shoot another big hole in your security strategy. Cisco Systems recently published another alarming statistic, stating that large enterprises, on average, "use over 1,200 cloud services—over 98% of them are Shadow IT."

My first IT job was working in Production Control at McNeil Consumer Products, just outside of Philadelphia, PA. My responsibilities involved moving large COBOL programs, on an IBM mainframe computer, into production. It was a big deal.

Programming teams, each comprised of five or six people,

---

[2] 2016 Garter Cloud Security Report

supported various applications throughout our company, including financial, manufacturing, marketing, R&D, etc.

Once a program was written, it was tested. Testing could take up to six months. Programs were tested for performance, integrity, stability, etc. Today, there would be serious time given to security. Once the testing teams had finished their work and signed off, it came to me. My job entailed writing the code to allow the mainframe to actually run the program in a production environment. It required mainframe access that only designated computer operators had. To reach the computer room, I needed several levels of access. Unless you had full access, you would never reach my cubicle.

It took months to go through testing, sign-off, and the production control process. Finally, the new program would be up and running, and end-users would be given access to begin using it. The point is, it was a well-thought-out, meticulous process, with many levels of control.

The Days of Testing Code Are Over

Today, that's all changed. An employee needs something; it might be a better browser, a time tracking program, a business card scanner, or a new exercise tracking program. Click on the app store icon, and run a quick search. Three or four options come up. The user is not sure which one is best, so they review the ratings. Two stand out, so they download them.

In another scenario, the user walks into a convention. It may be work or personal, but there's an app. Scan the poster and the event app pops up to download. The user hits go, and boom, it's loaded.

No thought is given to who actually created that app or whether or not it's secure. It might even be botware. What's to stop someone from printing off scan codes that download a bot, and pasting them over the real scan code in your local store or convention center? Without special mobile security software, that user has just given their electronic life over to someone they don't know.

I Make My Own IT Choices: Shadow IT

More on shadow IT. In the old days, people needed help installing applications and connecting to networks. Today, it's part of our everyday lives. Walk into Starbucks and connect. Check into a hotel and connect. Visit a city with public Wi-Fi and connect.

Computers, in whatever shape or size, come preconfigured to connect and go. In most cases, the user needs no networking experience. All devices seem like they are designed to connect to anything that wants a connection, good or bad.

The assumption is that it's my device, I'm in a hurry, and I know what I am doing. After all, it's my phone or tablet.

With this new mindset evolving, the end-user starts thinking they are the IT department. Suddenly it doesn't have to be a phone. It can be a laptop or company issued desktop. The more savvy your end-users are when it comes to computing, the more technology decisions they'll start making. Assume the younger employees were raised on computers and believe they know as much or more than the IT group. Chances are they even resent being told what to use, or how to do their job.

On the one hand, this may be more efficient. On the other hand, few IT people, let alone end-users, really understand security and risk. The likelihood of them making wise choices, when it comes to keeping data secure, is low at best.

Examples Close to Home: Security and the Shadow IT Threat?

Hillary Clinton's Gmail Fiasco

Perhaps the most notable instance of Shadow IT is Hillary Clinton's Gmail account. Regardless of your political party affiliation, or who you think should have won the US Presidential election, Hillary not only violated government security policies, she broke the law. She is one more example of Shadow IT, opening doors at the highest levels of security (Note: at the time of this writing, government officials had decided not to prosecute, but the FBI's description of what they found does describe a violation of what the current federal law demands).

It all started with the choice to not use the US government-issued email address assigned to her. Typical of Shadow IT, she allegedly used this email, setting it up with a personally registered domain, for easier accessibility. Much of the Shadow IT used in business today is simply to avoid cumbersome security login procedures, or to avoid corporate oversight. In this case it could be either or both. By using her Gmail account, Hillary circumvented the Federal Records Act which retains records of all correspondence.

Over a four year period, Hillary used her personal email account, while working for the State Department. Her staff did not make backups of her correspondence, which explicitly violates the law. By doing this, she not only avoided accountability, but also made it impossible for the US government to ensure that her communications were secure.

Recent reports now say that her email was in fact compromised. A hacker identifying himself as "Guccifer" reportedly released emails pertaining to Benghazi; emails exchanged between Clinton and Sidney Blumenthal. If you're not familiar with the specifics of Benghazi, it's a disaster. Of course no one seems to agree on anything, but had the rules on email been followed, the issue might not be so messy.

Your Personal Healthcare is at Risk

If you're a doctor, your patients may be at risk. If you're not, you and your family are likely at risk. Electronic medical records, mandated by President Obama are far from secure. So who's watching your data, and what can they learn from your medical history? Medical data is worth a lot of money. If anything is digital money, it's healthcare data.

Every day, doctors send and receive text messages on personal devices (BYOD).[3] Only about 11% use secure messaging, according to recent reports. Perhaps 50% have a basic understanding of data security. The rest don't. The general understanding is that, HIPAA compliance ensures security, but the actual risk of patient data compromise is unknown. 30% of doctors surveyed admitted that they were also receiving texts from patients containing private healthcare information. While this is a violation of HIPAA regulations, it's also a breach that is leading to fraud and impacting the lives of real people.

New York Presbyterian Hospital and Columbia University Medical Center are two good examples. Between the two of them, breaches cost about $4.8 million dollars in fines. Using a personally owned computer, one doctor at Columbia managed to expose 68,000 patients simply by misunderstanding data security best practices. This breach was discovered when a patient found their deceased partner's data posted online!

Who's at Risk?

You can't stop the BYOD movement. It's everywhere, and most likely it is taking shape in your company, even if you don't know it. The smartphone is an example; and who in your company doesn't have one?

Even if your current company policy is, "We don't allow it," end-users are going to do it. If you block it, they'll find a way around it. I've assessed many network environments and found all kinds of work-arounds. In one case, working with a global

---

[3] FAAS Healthcare Study 2016

pharmaceutical company, we discovered an entire global VAX Network (the now defunct Digital Equipment's mainframe and network technology). While a VAX network is not BYOD, it's that same mindset; I am my own IT.

In a recent study conducted by Cisco Systems, corporations were found to have nearly twice as many cloud applications in production as the IT department had a record of. In this case the department is purchasing cloud-based software, outside of IT's involvement. They're using their own stuff. I believe the entire BYOD movement will lead to more of these types of purchases as people see opportunities to build their business, but don't want to wait on IT. So who is at risk?

- ☐ **Small Businesses Operating Without an Internal IT Group**. If your company doesn't have a dedicated IT department, chances are you're lacking the necessary security policies, guidelines, and standards to operate securely. If that is the case, your top performers may be encouraged to go out and find what works, without any oversight, or a proper understanding of what makes something secure.

- ☐ **Mid-sized Companies With Very Small IT Departments**. A small IT group is often just as bad as not having one. If your team can't get the support they need, they'll grasp at whatever looks good, and use it.

- ☐ **Enterprises With Overly Strict or Out of Touch CIOs**. In the case of larger companies, the CIO role is being pushed into more of an innovator. If your company has not done this, your CIO may be old-school, meaning they are imposing restrictions without considering what knowledge workers really need to compete. Do this, and you can expect them to start building the proverbial VAX network.

- ☐ **Companies Not Adequately Equipping Their Knowledge Workers**. If for some other reason (budget comes to mind) your knowledge workers don't have what they need, they'll find another way to get it.

- ☐ **Companies That Have Educated Their End-Users on Security**. Looking back at Clinton, either she didn't know, or didn't care about security. We don't know which. But if she was in this role for several years, which is the case, someone should have realized that her email address was personal. Why didn't someone report it? Did they just not know what to do about it? Or were they unwilling?

- ☐ **Employees Who Lack Integrity**. Even if the user knows what to do, they may believe there is a better way, not fully understanding the security issues at hand.

Steps You Can Take to Reduce Your Exposure Due to Shadow IT

The best thing you can do is limit your exposure by clarifying how and when these devices should be used and managed. Rather than drawing a hard line in the sand, educate your team on the risks, and provide a more secure way to use BYOD. A few things you can do that won't cost you an arm and a leg:

- ☐ **Policies Limit Your Liability**. Your security policy should state what can be accessed by phone, who owns the data, and what happens when an employee leaves. But remember, un-enforced policies become recommendations over time. So make sure your policies are enforceable. I recommend contracting with someone who really knows security policy development practices to make sure you have what you need. Your policy should be clear: company data belongs to the company, regardless of who's device it sits on.

- ☐ **Require Your Users to Have Mobile Security Software**. Mobile security software programs are affordable and available for most BYOD devices. You can even carve off a section of a tablet for corporate use. When the employee leaves, that area of the phone can be wiped, leaving the rest intact. It might be wise to limit your liability here in case you somehow accidentally delete personal data. Require your user to back up their phone first.

☐ **Use NAC**. If possible, use NAC (Network Access Control) technology to enforce certain policies such as software updates, prior to connecting. Remember, policies don't secure. But you can use technology to enforce certain policies.

☐ **Provide Ongoing User Awareness Education**. Your users need to know what rogue access points are and why they are bad, what malware looks like, and what other BYOD software threats are trending. These won't always be obvious.

☐ **Your Leadership Team Should be Enabling the Company Technologically**. If you use an outside provider, you may need to increase your support contracts to include Virtual CIO services (vCIO). vCIO offerings have gained popularity over the past few years. Few companies can continue to grow without someone guiding them on the use of, or investment in, new technology.

CHAPTER SIX

Threat Three: The Social Media Craze

Social media is a paradigm shift that's here to stay. You would be surprised to hear how much people you've never met can know about you: neighbors, employers, marketers and …criminals. Underestimate this and you could lose everything.

Facebook is everywhere. Social media is here to stay. It's likely that both you and your kids are using Facebook, blogs, and other platforms for both personal and business use. Like BYOD, I'm not against social media. But there are some serious mindset changes that are exposing more data than you can imagine.

Remember twenty years ago, if you're old enough to have been using computers back then? It was the mid 90s the Internet exploded into personal and business use. Websites started popping up everywhere, and early social platforms like MySpace became popular. But it was scary to put pictures and articles online. Video was new, remember? No one wanted you to record them on video or even audio. We just weren't used to hearing our own voices, or seeing ourselves in motion. Putting a family picture online was not on my list of things to do.

Social media has changed all of that. People have no problem making funny videos, recording goofy actions, or writing blog posts about stupid things they've done. It's gone so far that many, young and old, send naked pictures of themselves to friends and significant others. It's unthinkable.

Understanding the Social Media Threat

Studies show that a lot of time is wasted on social media. Shopping is even worse. It is reportedly the number one time waster at work.

While wasted time should be a concern, stealing time from the employer is not my primary concern. There are tools out there to track the time people spend shopping and using social media platforms, and if you suspect your employees are abusing the Internet, it might be time to invest in software to both track and limit access.

But there's something much bigger at stake here. It's a mindset that is quickly evolving, removing our natural desire for privacy.

Social media platforms want people to share their secrets. The more people share, the more social media grows. They're counting on the unintentional release of confidential information by creating the illusion of intimacy and privacy. Facebook calls them *friends*, Google+ has circles, and Snapchat encourages the transmission of secret messages by claiming to delete your stuff soon after you send it. But none of this is truly private.

All of us are slowly losing that heightened sense of privacy that keeps us from sharing things that would expose us in ways that could negatively affect our reputation.

It's becoming an addiction. Once hooked on the practice of posting, we share more and more information without thinking about what we are sharing.

The Social Media Mindset: Sharing My Life With Strangers

Something very interesting is happening. When the face-to-face interaction goes away, so do the inhibitions. If you're married, you may not remember the dating scene all that well, but it's likely that you do remember it was hard to meet someone you would actually share your secrets with.

Along comes social media and online dating. I know several people who have met their spouses online. However, overall, I hear the relationship often breaks down when the people meet. Online, the sharing is easy. But once you're there in person, it gets harder.

People started out in the early days of MySpace sharing a few pictures and some tidbits about themselves. With 1.59 Billion Facebook users, social media is fast becoming the place people go to first when they get online. Snapchat is another fast growing platform with its own built in security feature. Once the picture is taken and sent, it can only be viewed one time, and after 10 seconds or less, it's deleted. The point is, it won't get passed around unless someone does a screen shot. And even then, the sender will be notified.

The problem with all of this is that social media platforms are somehow encouraging an age of exhibitionism, voyeurism, and a disregard for anything that used to be considered highly personal. Data is becoming easier to share, whether it's about you or your company.

Facebook is Using You

The truth is, Facebook and other platforms are encouraging this open sharing. Why? It's data. It's money.

Facebook is free, right? How did they become a $75 billion dollar company with no products and no inventory? They have data, and data is simply a form of digital money. Think of your data as a cybercurrency. It's worth a lot of money, even if you don't think it's that interesting. 85% of that $75 billion came from selling advertising. All day and night, you and everyone you know are posting data on Facebook pages. You "Like" things, search, click on ads, and contribute to other sites who just might sell your data to Facebook. What Facebook doesn't know about you, they will figure out through some very advanced data algorithms.

I will talk more about data aggregation later, but at the heart of profiling data sits social media, and a new, open-sharing mindset that is giving others everything they need to exploit, manipulate, and actually become the new you.

"Bobby is suddenly taken aback when the lending agent
doesn't understand his net worth calculations"

How Facebook and Other Sites Track and Learn All About You

Taking this one step further, data aggregation is quickly becoming the key to successful marketing. Not only is Facebook collecting and selling your data, but they are putting tools on your computer to track your habits! This should be illegal. But it's not.

It's not just Facebook. Google, Twitter, LinkedIn, they all do this because they can.

It starts with a cookie. You've heard of these. Are they bad?

There are many situations where you want a site to remember who you are so that you don't have to keep entering your information to buy or even login. But let's look at what is really going on.

When a person clicks on Facebook or LinkedIn, (or almost any site these days), a cookie is installed. Then, as the user moves on to other sites, that cookie keeps track of the sites visited, creating a repository of data. They're tracking your search habits over the course of the day.

In some cases, a survey is presented, collecting more data about how you think. This is called *seeding*. Often, the owner of the survey will not be revealed. It's just an online survey, so people do it. They're adding to their profile.

Cookies take this a step further with a technology called *Cookie-Syncing*. With your cookie installed, it will actually call out to other sites, exchanging marketing data to drive more ads to your screen. These tools are powerful enough to figure out what you are most likely to respond to. As time goes on marketers are getting better and better at getting you to buy things you don't need. Not only that, but given a clear understanding of your profile, a site can actually predict what price you will pay, changing the price for something like an airline ticket to get the most out of you.

Another interesting tool, called *Canvas Fingerprinting*, might be used to discover things about your computer. Using this technique, the website you're visiting will create an image that your computer will respond to. How it responds tells the site what OS you're running and more. If they know you are working on a Mac, you can expect to get more ads relevant to the Mac user.

Social Media Attacks Work Through Social Engineering.

With advancements in data aggregation and profiling comes the power of social engineering. The people around you fall into one of several categories. Some are lonely, some are going through hard times, some are addicted to something, and some are doing something unethical or illegal. I could go on. The bottom line is, there are lots of people around you with secrets.

There are also helpful people. Being helpful is admirable. For example, the worker who wants to get it all done before the day is over, or the employee who cares about the people around them, and is willing to do things that seem good, but which are not necessarily safe.

Social engineering figures out where a person is likely off guard. Some are hiding something, some are helpful to a fault, and some are simply too busy to ask questions. Once they understand the persona of their victim, the rest is easy. It's psychology and manipulation. If I want to get into a hotel back door, I can simply stand there reading my email until someone comes along with a card. The chances of them being rude enough to ask me for my ID or hotel access card are slim. We just don't do that sort of thing.

Social media is that kind of platform. It's a place to meet new friends, exchange ideas, and build trust. Anyone involved in social media eventually becomes an easy target. Some may take longer than others, but just about anyone can be duped with the right strategy and enough time.

If your employees use social media (and they do), it's just a matter of time before some unethical manipulator comes along to prey on them. Will they give up their personal data or your company data, probably both. After all, in their mind, there is no distinction.

Examples Close to Home: Using Social Media

Social media just might be your biggest security hole. Let's take a look at some real examples.

If They Send Out Their Naked Pictures, What Else Will They Send?

If someone will send out a picture of themselves, what else will they send? Can you trust this person with corporate data?

In a recent Wall Street Journal article, the writer described an investment company on Wall Street that was targeted by a 25 year-old woman on Facebook. Over a six month period, she managed to "Friend" most of the men in that organization. The report goes on to reveal that over 70% of them gave her highly sensitive financial information. But get this: 13% of the men handed her the passwords to the investment systems!

The breach was announced when the company leadership disclosed "her" as a hired, white-hat hacker, a 40 year old male they had contracted with to test the integrity of their team. How can a company defend against this type of attack? These are authorized users doing unauthorized things. It's a crime that is much harder to stop than an outside hacker breaking into your servers.

When Things Go Wrong on Social Media, it Can be Unexpected and Disastrous

One hot-headed response or thoughtless comment can backfire or quickly become negative. In today's cyberworld, it's almost impossible to keep a leash on what every employee is saying on social media. Here I've listed several posts or tweets that mistakenly disclosed corporate secrets.

☐ Netflix, CEO Reed Hastings, posted a congratulations on Facebook exposing their next strategic move…, Hastings wrote "Congrats to Ted Sarandos and his amazing content licensing team…When *House of Cards* and *Arrested Development* debut, we'll blow these records away. Keep going, Ted, we need even more!…"

☐ The chief of the British secret service MI6 was exposed when his wife posted details on Facebook, including their home address and names of close friends, complete with photos!

☐ Rep. Peter Hoekstra, a congressman and member of The House Intelligence Committee, gave away his secret trip to Iraq. Tweeted messages revealed his arrival in Baghdad, his itinerary, and his whereabouts throughout his trip.

☐ A secret mission was jeopardized when an Israeli soldier posted the location and time of an upcoming raid on Facebook.

☐ McDonalds, back in 2012, set up a hashtag for users to promote their favorite fast food restaurant through social media. If they'd been asked in person, chances are they would have given great feedback, or no comment. Instead, using hashtag #mcdstories, users submitted their horror stories! Backfire.

☐ During the first presidential debate prior to President Obama taking office, Kitchen Aid tweeted: "Obamas gma even knew it was going 2 b bad! She died 3 days b4 he became president. #nbcpolitics." Talk about bad branding!

It's easy to do. In seconds, your company can be demoralized, hated, or subject to lawsuits and fines, simply because someone wasn't thinking, and posted sensitive information to the world.

Who's at Risk?

Just about everyone uses social media. As I've pointed out in the examples above, executives, soldiers, government officials, they're all making mistakes with social media. It's an easy mistake to make. And the more comfortable we get with sharing personal stuff online, the worse it will become.

But not all people groups pose the same level of threat. A recent Wall Street Journal article noted that, "The millennial generation is particularly promiscuous with data." This reinforces my point. The longer you use social media, the looser you'll become with "classified data." The next generation will be even more so if trends continue. The article went on to say that millennials consider their information to be online and exposed anyway, so there's no reason to worry about it.

If you start telling people they can't use social media, they'll either ignore you or quit. Social media has become a mainline form of communication. It's also becoming central to marketing and customer service, and there's much talk about platforms like Facebook becoming more prominent as the user's primary search engine. You can't ignore or remove it. So who is at risk...?

- ☐ If your team isn't clear on what information is top secret, your risk is growing every day.

- ☐ Companies that don't classify data are at risk. If the user doesn't know what data matters, they are likely to treat it all as public information.

- ☐ When everyone knows the company secrets, those secrets will get out, especially when those secrets are fun to share. Secrets such as a new product announcement or juicy gossip are hard to keep secret.

- ☐ If you don't have technology in place to block certain transmissions or at least monitor activity, you can be sure people are leaking information. Even if it's out of ignorance, in an effort to get the job done faster.

Steps You Can Take to Reduce Your Exposure on Social Media

Chances are, you can't stop people from using social media, especially if they work from home or on the road. But remember, this is a leadership mindset problem. The right education and leadership can go a long way towards minimizing your risk.

☐ If you believe your team is wasting time, install tools at the gateway to monitor this type of activity. You might be surprised how much time people spend, not just on Facebook, but on shopping, sports sites, pornography, and even gaming sites. But remember, wasted time is not your biggest threat.

☐ Educate your team on how hackers talk users into giving up data and passwords (social engineering). The white hat hacker, referenced earlier, had her victims convinced she was their friend, and perhaps this could go further. Once trusted, they were willing to give her everything. And no one questioned whether she was real or not. In the end, it was a man. You never know who you're really dealing with online.

☐ Set up policies and awareness training. Your data should be classified according to sensitivity. Your people should be well educated on the need for security, and the deception that so easily entangles them. Don't underestimate this danger.

☐ Limit access to sensitive data. The less people know, the less likely it is to be posted.

☐ Deploy data leakage technology to keep sensitive information from leaving your office. Policies alone will never work. Like the examples above, it's just too easy to make a mistake when you're busy.

CHAPTER SEVEN

Threat Four: People Open Security Doors

> We feel much safer than we actually are. In many ways, we live in a society based on trust. You expect suppliers to keep their word. You expect your paycheck to cash. You expect your banker to accurately report your balance. But we all underestimate what cybercriminals will do for money, thrills, or religious belief. Social engineering may be your biggest threat.

At night, I lock my doors. As I drift off to sleep, I'm not thinking about home invasions. My neighborhood is pretty safe. We trust each other. If I really thought someone was going to break in, I would do much more than lock my door.

In my college days, safety was a real issue. Having grown up in the suburbs of Long Island, far enough from New York City to feel safe in our middle class neighborhood, we didn't think much about break-ins. But Drexel University, where I studied computer science, was a different story. My third-floor apartment, eight blocks north of the school, was hardly considered student housing. In the first week of school, one of my classmates was brutally murdered outside the computer lab late one night. The bloodstains on the city sidewalk were a daily reminder to us all.

After that incident, I was suddenly on the alert walking to and from my apartment. During the summer nights, we would have our windows open in hopes of some small breeze to cool us off. I had heard about robberies in our area, and soon realized that the three story climb to my window was not so insurmountable. If the kids on the block suspected that we had computers in our apartment, which of course we did, we were a target. Our home was not secure, and I was fearful.

Then one night, it happened. It was around 3:00 AM. I was suddenly stirred by an unexpected movement in my room. Only a silhouette could be seen between my bed and the window. Within seconds, my adrenaline kicked in and I was on my feet, throwing the perpetrator to the floor. My response was fast and furious. Subconsciously I knew it was either me or him; I had to disable this person.

But as I continued pounding my victim, it suddenly occurred to me, this was my roommate. I had been in a deep sleep, probably dreaming about our neighborhood. My poor roommate was simply getting up to use the restroom.

Looking back it seems funny, but at the time, it was traumatic for both of us. Jokingly, I told my roommate not to get up in the middle of the night any more. But inside, I was shaking, full of fear and adrenaline. For weeks, I would lie awake at night listening for suspicious sounds, waiting for something to happen.

Had this been an actual break-in, I now understand that my detection plan was too slow, and that my response probably would not work. Had this person been armed, I would have died.

Security has a lot to do with people. What people want, what they'll do, and how we secure ourselves to provide greater protection.

Two months later, following graduation, I moved south to a rather safe area outside the city of Charlotte, NC. But even in the south, it took months to convince myself that everything was okay. I now understand, from just one, brief encounter, why police officers have trouble sleeping.

Understanding the People Threat

We trust people. Especially when they live with us, work with us, or do business with us. When we meet someone we really don't trust, we avoid them. But it's not hard for someone to be convinced, duped into something they later regret.

A few years ago, I met Greg (not his real name) on a church men's retreat. His story was eye-opening. Early in life he had never really had success with dating, yet he longed to marry. Feeling somewhat hopeless, he decided to try online dating.

Not long into it, he met a woman from China. Over the next few weeks, they got to know each other, and their relationship began to take shape. Over the months they grew closer, and finally, he agreed to make a trip out to her hometown. He met her parents, spent time with her, and grew to love her.

After a few trips, they agreed to marry. The plan was for her to move to the U.S. and become a citizen through her marriage to Greg. Finally, Greg was married. Not long after, they had a child, and everything seemed to be going well. Until one day, when Greg was suddenly rudely awakened.

That evening, he came home from work, expecting to greet his lovely wife and child. They were gone. There was a note thanking him for all he had provided, but no details on where they had gone.

For over a year Greg searched in vain to find her, but she was nowhere to be found. In the end, it turned out that she had used Greg to gain her US citizenship. Once fully integrated in the States, she was on to another life. How could Greg have known ahead of time that this woman was not who she said she was? How much more likely is a deception when there are no physical interactions?

Our society is built on trust for the most part. I perform a service, send an invoice, and expect to get paid. If I sit down at a restaurant, they serve me before I pay (unless I'm eating fast food.) After I eat, I hand over my credit card, and allow them to process the charge in the back (something restaurants should change). When someone makes a request in the office, even if it's someone you don't know, from another division, the assumption is, they are who they say they are. Most of us will go ahead and do the thing they've asked. Especially if their title carries some authority.

We all live with a false sense of security and a feeling that people are, in general, good.

The Truth About People

Most of us live in a sheltered world. Most of us have not had to live in a slum area like the one I lived in as a student. A small percentage of you have perhaps experienced the real evil a man is capable of. It might be domestic violence, child or sexual abuse, or perhaps you've been on active military duty and fought for your country. The horrors you've seen dwarf mine; ou really do understand.

My neighborhood is safe because I live among a small group of people who are pretty much like me. Families with children, jobs, plenty of food, and nice homes. I work with people like me, professionals who care about their reputation enough to pay their bills on time, and who desire to be in good standing with suppliers, as well as being seen as a responsible citizen in their community. Bottom line, we feel safe because we have not personally experienced horror.

We are All Connected; To Some of the Very Best, and Some of the Most Deranged People in the World

Whatever your experience, you are now connected to all kinds of people.

You're connected to the richest people on the planet, along with some of the poorest, (radicals and conservatives, anarchists, neo-Nazis, Mafia, communist governments, sovereign citizens who refuse to recognize government and law, and serial murderers.) You're connected to child molesters, abductors, and sexual predators, all of whom are just a click away. You're connected to people who love you, but also those who would kill you just for the fun of it, and watch you bleed for their own sexual satisfaction.

Scary, isn't it? Actually it's sick just to think about it.

You can't trust anyone you meet online. Electronically, a person can pretend to be anyone they want to be. Evil can truly be disguised as the angel of light. If you have no other means of knowing someone, be wary. Be vigilant. The fact is, anyone you meet online could be the opposite of what they say, or the picture they show. Even online video offers no proof. Nothing is as it seems without further proof. Take note: the sale of child pornography is the fastest growing industry online today.

This is how social engineering works. Collect data, make connections, build trust, draw the victim in, and get what you want while remaining anonymous.

Computer Security Can't be Trusted Either

That brings us to the topic of computer security. People are primarily driven by power, money, and sex. The Internet is the gateway to all three.

You've been told that passwords will keep your data safe, and that encryption will keep your data transmission secure. You've been told that chip and pin technology will guard your credit card, and that the FDIC will insure your digital money. You've been told firewalls will keep the bad people off of your network, and that your iPhone password will keep anyone from accessing your personal life. After all, the phone deletes itself after 10 wrong password guesses.

Everything you've been told about security is only partially true. Passwords keep your friends out. They don't stop hackers. Firewalls block the noise, but they don't stop hackers. Encryption makes your data harder to read, but it won't stop hackers from accessing you most sensitive information. Hackers don't really care about your security.

Our country is quickly going digital. Electronic medical records (EMR) are perhaps the biggest digital mistake, with regard to security, that our government has made in the past four years. Paper files can be lost in a fire, but they can't be accessed without making a personal visit to the office, and physically breaking into the file room. EMR connects every criminal named above to your personal data. How does that make you feel?

The Most Powerful Hacker Tool Out There: Social Engineering

Most of us trust data security. In many cases we just have to. Your bank is going to be digital, and there's nothing you can do about it. You also can't stop the government from moving your medical records to a digital system. It's there; there's nothing you can do about it. But don't be fooled, it's not secure.

Along with these so called advancements are recommendations to secure your data. The problem is *social engineering*. Greg was actually a victim of social engineering. His wife carried out a plan that took lots of patience, but seemingly had a big payoff for her in the end. By the way, she also drained their joint savings account before disappearing, which was perfectly legal as a joint account holder.

Social engineering is a people thing. When companies undergo security assessments to uncover vulnerabilities, they often leave out social engineering. They are just testing the technology. Yet, if you look back at the details of just about every major cybercrime event reported in the news over the past 12 months, you'll see that social engineering was central in almost every case.

Social engineering is simply the process of tricking people into doing something online to create an open door, providing access to secured data. It's a ruse used to get someone to do something they should not be doing, without the hacker actually having to do anything very technical in nature. The skills to hack through the firewall are suddenly no longer required.

So if your firewall vendor told you that your firewall would be nearly impossible to hack through, they're right. But how hard would it be to get one of your office workers to open an email, or even download a software patch? History has shown us it's not that difficult. I'm certain that I could convince half of your office workers to do it in a single day.

It's back to trust. If I call your office, drop some executive-level names, and claim to be a third-party IT support team for your company, or one of your new in-house IT administrators, chances are I can get your office workers to cooperate. After all, they don't want to be seen as difficult, and they probably do want to get back to their work so they can make it home to dinner on time.

Who Uses Social Engineering?

As I mentioned before, most of the successful breaches you've read about had some element of *social engineering*. It doesn't matter who the hacker is. It could be a nation or individual. They're using the same tools. The idea is to impersonate someone or provide an offer or service that sounds legitimate.

How Does Social Engineering Work?

Social engineering is usually part of a larger scam. Earlier, I mentioned bots, ransomware, and other unwanted software. Anything from an email that pretends to offer the status of a recent online order (Phishing email), to a phone call that pretends to be your service provider, could be a social engineering ruse.

In most cases they'll want you to do something. They may want you to click a link, download a software update, or grant access to your system to check or update something for you.

There have been many attempts like this that were written in poor English, requesting something unlikely (such as a request to wire money to a long lost uncle stranded in Germany). In most cases you won't fall for this, although some have. But today's phishing emails are getting better. It's getting much harder to tell what's real, and what isn't.

Examples Close to Home: Social Engineering

Do smart people really fall for these scams, or is it just the ignorant? Can someone send an email or make a phone call, and have your team of well-educated office workers open doors wide to hackers? Let's take a look at how this plays out.

Hacking One of the Largest Security Software Companies in the World

Even security companies are at risk. In 2011, RSA, now part of the EMC Corporation, was successfully hacked using social engineering to gain access. No one is above being hacked.

The irony here is that RSA is the author of SecurID, a well-known two-factor authentication technology used to prevent people from gaining access to secret data.

To date, many of the details of this breach have not been disclosed. However, we've been told that the hackers gained access to data that potentially made the SecurID technology less secure. Does that include source code? I don't know.

The ruse started with a series of emails with an Excel spreadsheet attached. The spreadsheet claimed to hold data regarding RSA's 2011 recruitment plan. These emails didn't go to IT personnel, or administrators with unrestricted access. Neither did they go to high-profile executives. They went to two small groups that apparently had access to data the hacker could use.

From news reports, we know that these emails actually went to a spam folder, probably due to the embedded macros contained in the attachment. Yet, the titles were enticing enough to get the office worker recipient to move it out of *trash*, review the contents, and allow the macros to run. Once open, a bot was installed, giving access to the perpetrator. In this case, an exploit that installed a backdoor through an adobe flash program (that has since been patched). The recovery cost? About $66 million!

Apple's First Official Ransomware Attack

In 2016, Apple reported its first full-scale ransomware attack. In this case, a ruse called water-holing was used. Rather than phishing with email, malware was planted on a legitimate website.

The attackers, likely working from China, managed to infect a popular file transmission software program used for bit torrent protocol transfers, a method of moving very large files such as movies and online games. Specifically, Transmission, a brand of bit torrent software, was attacked directly, adding ransomware to their version 2.90 download. Once downloaded, the software would then encrypt the user's hard drive after a three-day waiting period. Once encrypted, the user would be left to either restore from a clean back-up (if they had one), or pay the ransom.

A couple of important things to point out about this attack. Unlike the RSA attack, the Transmission software was legitimate. Hackers were able to infect the actual download in this case, making it nearly impossible for users to distinguish between something real, and a ruse. The download also came from the real Transmission site (versus a redirected site). In some cases, these attacks will be hosted on a similar site, catching those who mistyped the site name, or who get redirected to a fake site.

Hackers were requesting one bitcoin, or about $400 in ransom fees to unlock the data. Reports cited about 600,000 installs before the patch was applied and the ransomware stopped. In most cases, the downloaders were computer savvy. The average, non-technical person is probably not using bit-torrent protocols. Yet, they fell for it and paid the price.

Even Target's 110 Million Credit Card & Personal Data Record Loss Started with Social Engineering

"The breach at Target Corp. that exposed credit card and personal data on more than 110 million consumers appears to have begun with a malware-laced email *phishing* attack sent to employees at an HVAC firm that did business with the nationwide retailer," writes Brian Krebs, author of the well-known security new site, *Krebs on Security*.

While all of the details have not been disclosed, reports state that Target's HVAC contactor, Fazio Mechanical, was the victim of phishing attacks that used malware to steal passwords. Once equipped with Target's passwords, the skimming began.

In this case, a third-party supplier breach resulted in major losses to Target, as well as job losses for Target's CEO and CIO. (Note: the news reports did not directly link these job changes to the attack. However, my assumption, based on surrounding events, is that both positions were directly affected by this breach.)

Who's at Risk?

Social engineering is most common today with phishing attacks. The objective is to land keyloggers on someone's computer in hopes of stealing data, most likely credit card numbers that can be resold.

However, these attacks are evolving. Consider the following trends:

☐ Ransomware has doubled annually over the past four years. Phishing and waterhole attacks have proven to be the most effective way to land ransomware on a computer. From there, the payout rate seems pretty high (although companies often hide the fact that they were hit and paid the fee). Fees start around 1 bitcoin ($404), and have risen to amounts as high as 30 bitcoin, or about $20,000 USD. I expect fees to continue to climb over the coming years. Every company should be worried about ransomware, taking active steps to stop it before a ransom is requested.

☐ Any user who does not have a clear procedure for dealing with unsolicited tech support calls is wide open. Fake *tech support* groups are likely to contact your team through online pop-ups, email, or phone. Make sure your tech support procedures are well understood and consistent to avoid this ruse.

☐ If your spam filters are weak, you can expect more than half of the spam coming through to contain malware. The more professional these emails look, the more likely it is that your team will click on them.

☐ Is your company using third-party suppliers who have access to your networks? The weak link defines your security. Like Target, if your HVAC company hasn't taken security seriously, the attack will come through them.

☐ If your team uses social media, and does not understand how hackers use these platforms, they will likely expose your company through their own, personal, online interactions. Downloading something personal from a Facebook link can be just as damaging as opening an email from hackers in Russia.

Steps You Can Take to Reduce Your Exposure

Whatever you put in digital form is accessible from anywhere in the world by someone who knows how to get to it. Social engineering may be the first step in accessing yours. But there are some things you can do to limit your exposure to social engineering.

☐ First, there is one big mistake that individuals and companies are making with security today. I address this in detail in Part II, so rather than explaining it here, keep these ideas in mind as you read through the next section of the book.

☐ Education and end-user awareness training are an important step to securing data. If your team is at least aware of what's happening, they'll be more vigilant when something doesn't sound right. Social engineering hackers often make mistakes in the way they talk, phrase things, or describe things. Listen carefully. Ask questions. Demand accurate answers.

Don't trust anyone online until they've proven to be trustworthy.

☐ Use Google. The computer is sitting in front of us when the hacker approaches. When someone claims to be Apple Support, it's easy to verify by asking a few key questions you can find answers to online. In a two-minute conversation, I was able to find out that a support person was in fact a scammer when he claimed to be offering support for Apple users out of India.

☐ Two-factor authentication requires something you have and something you know. By using a token, hackers might have your password, but they don't have your token.

☐ Keep up with your security policies and procedures. You can often cut off these hackers by stating policies and procedures regarding how tech support is handled, what information can be given out by phone or email, and what to do when a request is made that falls outside of these parameters. For instance, banks will never send you a link to update your information. But the user needs to know that if they are to avoid being scammed.

☐ When contacted by an outside support group asking for something special (like access to your computer, or a payment of some kind), have your people call back the company's main number. This same practice should be carried out at home as well. For instance, is someone calling to get payment for an outstanding phone bill? Hang up and call the phone company directly.

CHAPTER EIGHT

Threat Five: The Threat Around You, Co-workers

> Even if your walls and fences could keep the bad guys out, the person sitting in the office next to you has access. Recent surveys report that 75% of employees steal from their employer. The other 25% are lying.

Years ago, working at one of the largest banks in our nation, my team was informed that a temp. working for one of the telecom managers was suspected of belonging to a crime ring. After some digging, it turned out to be true. She was immediately taken into custody and charged. To my knowledge, her colleagues were not caught. She claimed she was acting alone. The truth is, she was willing to serve time rather than rat out her team.

A few years later, my immediate director was charged with fraud for purchasing computer equipment through the IT organization and selling it on the black market. Across the street, a well-known global networking company discovered that their regional sales team was booking fake business and getting paid on it.

Internal theft is more common than you might think. I have frequently recommended to small businesses, that if they have a financial person on staff, they should be monitoring that computer system. There are software programs out there that monitor key strokes, take screen shots of predefined activities, and alert you to things you've asked to be notified about. Not long ago, one of my longtime clients and I were talking about this. I asked him if he'd ever thought about doing this with his controller. She was a longtime friend of my client's family, and it was hard for him to think that she might be doing anything illegal. But after some pressuring, he decided to do it. Neither of us had any reason to believe there was a problem, but just to be prudent and kill his curiosity, he moved forward with some monitoring software. Sure enough, she was stealing from him.

There's been a long-standing debate as to whether the insider or outsider threat is greater. I have my opinions, but they are just that, an opinion. In this chapter I'll address some things to be thinking about, and some steps of action to minimize your risk.

Understanding the Internal Threat

Rarely will a company give their financial people full authority to write and sign checks. There's just too much temptation. When cashiers end their day, they balance their cash box before leaving. Tellers do the same. Why? It's not because no one trusts anyone… well, sort of. Managers and business owners know that money is a big motivator. And when someone is short on money, or in financial trouble, they will steal, even from their friends.

In business, you don't know who your friends are. Employees are hired off the street. A background check might be run, along with a drug test in some businesses. After that, it's a trust relationship. That person may be trustworthy, but people and circumstances change, and easy money is a big temptation.

It's prudent, not over protective, to put controls in place. For instance, having a limit on signing checks and budget approval authority is common practice. As money becomes more and more digital these types of controls become more important. And remember, much of your data carries with it value, just like cash, so keep an eye on it. Unfortunately, many business leaders have discovered this too late, and they've been taken.

The internal threat comes in many flavors. It's not easy to stop someone internally or to detect intrusions. Especially if they have authorized access for their job. Here are a few things to watch out for:

Accidental Data Exposure and Operational Error

Some security issues are an accident. Unstructured data placed on a SharePoint server or website, without the proper security, may expose social security numbers, salaries, or other classified information to unauthorized users internally, or out on the Internet. This happens all the time, simply because the users have access to query and download the data, but don't understand where they are putting it.

Disaster recovery specialists agree that about 40% of downtime is actually due to operational errors. So this security issue may be data exposure, but it could also be data loss or lack of availability. All of these are security issues.

Taking Data with Them When They Leave

When a sales person leaves, heading off to a new sales position, it's common for them to take their data with them. In fact, job boards even post requirements for a new position including "a large Rolodex." This data belongs to the company, not the individual sales person. Yet the new employer is expecting the sales candidate to bring that data with them. What will happen when that new sales representative goes to their next position with a competitor?

The same would be true for those working in R&D labs, project management, or just about any professional job. If they've been gathering data and doing something with it for ten years, chances are they feel it's their right to take their work with them. It is pretty hard to stop this sort of thing. Yet, contractually all of this data does belong to the employer.

Unauthorized Activity, by Authorized Users

Authorized users are required to work on sensitive and controlled data. This would be the case with any computer operator who administers the systems that control bank accounts. How hard would it be to add some code to skim off a few cents on every transaction?

Banks know this, so generally there is a division of responsibilities. In other words, you can't write and sign the check. A second signature is required. But in many situations, this is not the case. End-users may have access to all kinds of data including health records, credit card numbers, and other data that is easily sold on the black market. Again, this is pretty hard to detect.

When someone steals a physical object from your home, you know it's missing. But when someone steals your data, it's still there. It's just a copy that's been taken. And if it's in the person's job description to access and use that data, they haven't done anything wrong until they actually sell it, or give access to an unauthorized user (or put it somewhere that violates your security policy).

Planted by Outside Crime Rings

It takes time and patience, but if the data is worth enough, crime rings and governments will insert people into the system from the outside. This was the case with several terrorist operations including the 9/11 attacks. These pilots were authorized, despite their criminal intent. The woman caught in the crime ring at the bank was the same.

How hard would it be to have someone trained in a specialized field such as aeronautical engineering, only to insert them into the US space program, with orders to leak information? The same is happening in all areas of business and government right now. It just requires some patience and training. Again, these types of infiltrations are very difficult to detect and stop before it's too late.

Hired by Outside Hackers

This last one, hired by hackers, might be one of the biggest problems. Here you have someone working for your company without ill intent. But how many of your employees would give in if enticed by an offer to make some big money, tax free?

Think about it. They don't have to break into an office, or kill anyone. It might be as simple as relaying a password or downloading a file to a server.

Some reports I've read tell the story of cybercrime gangs paying up to ten times more than an IT worker's current salary for the right access. When the average pay increase is in the single digits (2-4%), and the economy is unstable, the temptation might just be too much for the average IT employee with a growing family and bills to pay.

Examples Close to Home

It's an ongoing debate. Is the internal threat bigger? Or is the outside hacker more dangerous? The biggest hacks we read about are external. There's no doubt in my mind. However, there are some big ones on the inside. It's also true that most employees steal from their employer. Studies show this to be true, and it makes sense. Let's look at the devastation that occurs when insiders take matters into their own hands, or when the wrong insiders are allowed in.

The Edward Snowden Case

He was part of the NSA (National Security Agency.) Right or wrong, I'm not here to debate. The fact is, it could have been Coke or Michelin Tires' recipe. But what he did was against the law.

Snowden was an unknown name just a few years ago, now famous for leaking information from his agency. Reports cite as many as 1.7 million documents were exposed by Snowden. Wikipedia states that, "The vast majority of those documents were related to our military capabilities, operations, tactics, techniques, and procedures." Reports from Britain also claim that Snowden's intelligence leaks, "negatively impacted Britain's ability to fight terrorism and organized crime."

While Snowden believed his actions were justified, the fact is, he was not on board with his organization's directives, and therefore felt justified in disclosing secret information. My concern is that, given the political divisions taking place around the world right now, just about any employee could decide their company's moral and political positions justify some criminal act. Whatever your company stands for, you want to make sure your team is on board, and not working to destroy you. A disgruntled employee, with conviction, can totally destroy everything your company is working toward.

Leaking Space Shuttle Secrets to China

Several years ago a Chinese engineer at Boeing was convicted of spying; leaking secrets to China. Dongfan "Greg" Chung, a citizen of the US, was convicted of economic espionage, acting as an agent for the People's Republic of China.

His plea: *innocent*. He claimed he loved America and was not spying. However, during a home search, Federal Agents discovered over 300,000 pages of sensitive documents relating to the space shuttle, Delta IV rocket, F-15 fighter, B-52 bomber, CH-46/47 Chinook helicopter, and other aerospace and military technologies.

Chung was sentenced to 15 years in prison. However, whatever was leaked to his colleagues in China can never be recovered. This type of attack takes patience, but when the payoff is big, terrorists and nation-states will spend years and millions of dollars to get what they want.

350,000 Accounts; Unauthorized Access

Morgan Stanley, the 2nd largest wealth manager in the country, had 10% of its wealth management clients affected when an employee took names and account data back in 2015. Nine hundred of those clients had their data posted online.

Morgan Stanley claims that no money was stolen, and that the employee was terminated. But the data was still exposed.

It is believed that the employee wanted to sell the information. However, the data put online was detected shortly after it was posted, stopping any sales from taking place.

While Morgan Stanley was able to stop this one, the likelihood of it happening again, somewhere else, is high. Especially with a smaller, less secure bank, or companies holding digital assets. Companies with assets that are highly valued on the black market, but who don't possess the technology needed to detect such a breach.

Small Business Accounting

Is your onsite financial person or bookkeeper reliable and trustworthy? I mentioned this one earlier, the controller stealing from her longtime friend and employer. It happens more than you think.

Unfortunately, when people are hurting and it comes to money, character often takes a back seat. What about your financial people? Can they all be trusted?

Who's at Risk

Internal threats come with different motivations. Depending on the types of data you have, and the state of your business, you may face different internal threats.

- ☐ Is your company struggling economically, perhaps going through a major outplacement initiative? Over the past two years, we've seen major companies laying off thousands of people. When this happens, people start grasping for anything they can use to make their next opportunity easier to find. Company secrets, client lists, financial reports, they're all up for grabs. In some cases, disgruntled employees will use technology to create "logic bombs" designed to destroy a company's computers once they are gone.

- ☐ If you work with any sort of classified data that might be helpful to Nation-States, expect them to be working on ways to access that data. They may do it using bots, but in more important cases, like that of Boeing, they'll insert someone local into the company to steal the data.

- ☐ Are there people in your company who have access to money, digital money, or something easy to turn into money? There probably are. Are any of them really hurting financially? If so, the temptation might just be too much. People working with highly-valued data need accountability.

- ☐ Is your company involved in a lawsuit? If so, you can expect whoever is on the opposing side to be looking for ways to get information on anything that might help their case. If this can be done by hacking or finding an insider to help, they just might do it.

☐ Hackers hire people with access; your employees. Believe it or not, hackers can get access to your IT people. Their resumes are online right now. Just about every one of them is looking for a new job if the price is right. What if that job opportunity pays 5 to 10 times more, but keeps them in their current role working for you? All they have to do is provide access to an outsider and they'll get paid. This is happening every day. It's hard to detect, and it's hard to stop. Chances are, you'll never catch them until they make a mistake.

Steps You Can Take to Reduce Your Exposure

The insider threat is real, and it won't be easy to uncover. But here are a few things you can start doing to minimize your risk.

☐ Separation of duties. Whenever possible, require more than one person to accomplish a task dealing with highly sensitive data. There should be checks and balances that create accountability just like the bank teller.

☐ Everyone should have their own password. If you don't know who is logging in, you can't track their activity. Require people to log in with unique credentials, and track their activities with logs and journals.

☐ SIEM technology can be used to track user activities. If authorized users are downloading massive amounts of data at 3:00 AM, and that's unusual, you'll want to be alerted.

☐ Insist on background checks and perform reviews of your users' computers and activities. This is especially hard with BYOD, but necessary.

☐ Restrict access to financial systems, ensuring that rights are set up to prohibit unauthorized activities.

☐ Be on the alert for disgruntled employees who might create problems in the systems they oversee. When someone is on their way out, be especially vigilant.

☐ Use two factor authentication to prevent administrators from accessing other's systems without their knowledge.

CHAPTER NINE

Threat Six: Other Nations Want Your Data

> We're losing this battle simply because the people creating and using data in your office don't understand the enemy, the weapons, the motivations, and the mistakes every one of us are making as we enter a digitalized world.

The newspaper is always blaming China, Russia, and sometimes North Korea when something goes wrong. These countries always deny it. It's clear that we are not at war with these countries, as I write this book (at least in the sense of ground troops and aerial bombings). So how valid are these accusations? Are other governments really in our systems? Is the US government really letting this kind of thing go on unchallenged?

Understanding the Nations-State Threat

There have been numerous hacker reports concerning the Chinese

Government over the past year. While I have not personally experienced these attacks, news reports are absolutely saying, "Yes."

"The disclosure in early 2015 of a secretive Chinese military unit believed to be behind a series of hacking attacks has failed to halt the cyber intrusions," according to Reuters's writers, Deborah Charles and Paul Eckert.

Wall Street published the above Chinese military article in November 2013, pointing to the People's Liberation Army, Shanghai-based Unit 61398, the primary suspect.

Wall Street's allegations sound pretty specific. What are they after? According to Reuters, this effort involves "cyber espionage to steal proprietary economic and trade information" from the US. In other words, they are after US innovation; stealing what has taken years to develop. Their plan is simple. They aim to take US innovations and manufacture them without the upfront R&D cost.

Expect these new products to come on the market for much less, competing with the inventor on price. This is called a *copycat* product. Copycat products are sold at a fraction of the price of the real product, and often put the inventor out of business.

If your clients are still thinking they are safe, have avoided attacks, and have *it covered* when it comes to keeping their innovation secrets under cover, they're likely out of touch with the real world. IT has often said, "*We have it covered*," only to later find out that hackers have been inside for years. Innovation is another form of *digital money*.

Your Country's Biggest Problem

Recently, US government officials have come out saying, "Cybersecurity threats are the greatest threat to our security; economic security, political security, diplomatic security, military security, etc." Note: this could be any country. No matter how big your business is, cybersecurity is something you want to understand and engage in.

So even if it's not your CIO's number one concern right this minute, these reports underscore the importance of security. Everyone out there has the need.

Examples Close to Home

Is this really happening consistently enough that we should be concerned? Isn't our government powerful enough to stop this? Don't these large companies have pretty strong security programs in place? Let's take a look and see just how big this is.

The Largest Bank Heist Yet: A Nation-State Sponsored Attack

In 2016, Kim Jong Un was blamed for stealing $81 Million from a Bangladesh bank, by exploiting the SWIFT system.

Kim is notorious for starving his people and funding his country through counterfeiting, drug trafficking, gun running, and slave labor, according to the WSJ reports. So hacking is certainly not out of the question.

Security researchers can often pick up patterns in malware. In this case, the code used on the attack looked a lot like that of the Sony hack just a year prior. It was likely a response to Sony's movie, which depicted Kim Jong Un in an unfavorable light and made fun of his policies and personalities.

While the US has promised to impose sanctions on North Korea, its ties to China make any serious repercussions unlikely. The important lesson here is, even though we would not expect governments to steal from banks around the world, this type of criminal behavior is taking place, at the government level, in more than one country. Stopping it is not as easy as you might think.

Following Are Some Hard Hitting News Quotes Regarding China:

"If the mission were to change, they [Chinese Hackers] have all the tools (speaking of cyberwarfare) in place to destroy…" - WSJ

"Chinese military unit 61398, is believed to be behind the theft of hundreds of terabytes of information from 141 organizations primarily in the United States." – SC Magazine

"Mandiant named the group APT1…it is only one of dozens of advanced persistent threat (APT) groups with China-based operations that the firm tracks." – WSJ

"Industries targeted by APT1 also match industries that China has identified as strategic to their growth,… identified in its 12th Five Year Plan." – Department of Homeland Security. (Reports show that this has been going on for 12 years, and that 12 major industries are targeted in these attacks.) – WSJ

"The size of APT1's infrastructure indicates that hundreds, and possibly thousands, of people work for this group, including linguists, open source researchers, malware authors, industry experts..." – Department of Homeland Security. – WSJ

"U.S. Eyes Pushback On China Hacking"

The above headline appeared in the CIO section of The Wall Street Journal this past year. One interesting perspective from the news reporter explains that these attacks are "small enough for our government to ignore them." In other words, there is no one single incident big enough to demand a government level response.

This is important. It's a way for one country to attack another without actually going to war. Another article in that same section warns us that, "All major US companies have been successfully compromised…" Where is this all headed?

Companies who insist, "They've got it covered…" are in trouble and kidding themselves. No company is impenetrable.

This is the problem with pen-testing. A successful pen test may show your security is good. But it actually delivers a false sense of security. While compliance laws often require these tests, a failure to break in really just shows the incompetence of the pen-testing team. It certainly doesn't mean the company is well secured.

In a recent report from the US President's office, we read, "The Obama administration is considering a raft of options to more aggressively confront China over cyberspying,…a potentially rapid escalation of a conflict the White House has only recently acknowledged." The key phrase here is, "Only recently." Why have government officials denied this for so long?

Perhaps for political and economic reasons. The Journal states it like this, "Before now, US government officials and corporate executives had been reluctant to publicly confront China out of fear that stoking tension would harm US national-security or business interests."

Why are the Chinese on the attack? "China is stealing trade secrets as part of plans to bolster its industry" (WSJ). Another way to say this is that the US has a greater capacity for innovation, and China, among others, wants access to it. By invading a company's intellectual capital, other nations can cut thousands of man-days out of the R&D process.

Google, EMC, RSA, New York Times, Wall Street Journal, and many other well-known companies, along with many federal organizations, including the Pentagon, have reported problems that can be traced back to China. However, things like "dependency on China to underwrite US debt and to provide a market for US businesses," have allowed these nation-state sponsored attacks to go largely unchallenged.

The FDIC: Hacked by China; Covered Up by US Officials

If all of that isn't enough to convince you, look at the July 13th, 2016 CNN Report on the FDIC hack. According to this report,

Chinese spies hacked FDIC (Federal Deposit Insurance Corp.) computers for three years, up until 2013. But it was never reported! Why?

A congressional report, published in 2016, states that government officials covered this up, keeping it from the media and the public eye. The report calls FDIC's bank regulators inept and deceitful. Twelve computers are reported as being compromised, along with ten servers, including, "incredibly sensitive personal computers of the agency's top officials; the FDIC Chairman, his chief of staff, and the general counsel."

The FDIC is the agency responsible for monitoring banks that are not reviewed by the Federal Reserve. In addition, this agency insures your deposits every time you put money in the bank. These computers contain highly sensitive information for over 4500 banks spread across the US.

Failure to disclose this hack was a violation of the FDIC's own policies and may very well have been illegal. Reports indicate that this may have been ordered internally for political reasons, such as to avoid jeopardizing their CEO's political future. The report goes on to say that it may be more common than we think for government agencies to hide these types of attacks from the public. Regardless of what you thought, insiders have said, "The Chinese are in all of our systems. Our only option is to try and keep them from getting to the most sensitive data."

Did Russia Break Into US Democratic National Convention Computers?

"The Democratic National Committee's (DNC) computer systems were compromised by hackers linked to the Russian government, in one of the largest known breaches of a US political organization," according to WSJ reports (June 2016).

According to the Crowdstrike, a security firm retained by the DNC, two groups with ties to the Russian intelligence services hacked the DNC systems. And apparently, this is not the first time.

Previous reports indicate that these same organizations had penetrated systems at the White House, State Department, and US Joint Chiefs of Staff.

This falls under the term, economic espionage. Monitoring DNC communications and accessing research on Presidential Candidate Donald Trump, Russian Government officials appeared to be keeping tabs on US elections and how they might affect Russia's future. Of course, Russia denies these allegations.

If they're in these systems, you can bet they're also monitoring more important systems such as the Department of Defense and Homeland Security. Additional Wall Street Journal reports say they are.

Who's at Risk?

Nation States probably don't care about your company's QuickBooks online data, or your customer list. However, they are looking for the digital money, in whatever form it might be.

- ☐ Innovations are important. Much of the US innovation comes from small businesses. These countries know they need innovation, and they also know they don't have it. Why? That's a whole different discussion. Assume that, if you have millions invested in R&D for something new (especially high-tech), someone overseas wants it. If you don't protect it, it will show up overseas as a copycat product with very little R&D investment.

- ☐ Money is always a target. As in Kim Jong Un's case, where digital money is at stake, you can believe that other nations will try to get it. The SWIFT system transmits over a trillion dollars every day. That's a target with a big payday.

- ☐ If you work with government, you might be a target. If the government systems are too hard to access, a subcontractor might be the ticket. If your company does subcontract work for any government agency holding military or defense secrets, or something else worth money, other governments want it. They may hack you, or insert an employee into your system. They'll get it somehow, unless you stop them first.

☐ The same is true if you do subcontract work for other large organizations such as Boeing, or a large bank, such as the Bank of Bangladesh.

Steps You Can Take to Reduce Your Exposure

These attacks are financially motivated and large in scale. They are after the possession of government data and intellectual capital that benefits their country. So the first step to managing risk is to evaluate your data. Do you have the kind of data they would want? If you're not well educated on security and digital value, you might consult someone who is before answering. Businesses often underestimate the value of their data. These attacks generally use one of two methods.

Planting Nation State Employees

We've already addressed insider threats, and that would be one of them. If you have data other nations want, then extra effort in screening new employees is needed. Regardless of compliance laws, make sure your new hires are not there on behalf of some foreign country. That might be impossible to tell for sure, but make every effort.

Putting in extra controls for monitoring activity and separation of duty all apply here.

Malware Attacks: Advanced Persistent Threats (APT)

The second method most commonly used is malware, along with social engineering to insert it. We covered this under Threat 1: Malware and Bots. I've added APT (Advanced Persistent Threats) here to underscore more sophisticated software attacks that may be harder to detect. Advanced, because they are more sophisticated and perhaps polymorphic (meaning they keep changing to avoid detection). Persistent, because when a nation state wants to get in, they'll keep working at it. Remember, people can always get in if they really want to. It's just a matter of time and patience.

In Part II, as I review the one big mistake most companies are making, I'll show you the best way to avoid this type of attack. And while technology is needed, it's not what you think. Before we get to that, let's cover one more major trend you'll need to be aware of in order to keep your digital money safe.

CHAPTER TEN

Threat Seven: A New Kind of War: Digital

Expect to see wars being fought online from terrorists, to nations fighting nations. The US has always been relatively safe, given the vast oceans that surround us. But these weapons travel that distance at the speed of light, virtually undetected.

Nation-State sponsored attacks are not meant to take yours or my country down. They are most often financially motivated. If the US stops innovating, it hurts those who are stealing from us. It's somewhat ironic, but you want your enemy to prosper when you make your living stealing from them. But Cyberwarfare is different, and more recently a threat.

Understanding the Cyberwarfare Threat

Cyberwarfare is different. In this case, unlike the other issues I've covered, the goal is destruction. Hacktivism, something I have not spent a lot time on, but which was a major trend back in the 2013 time frame, is the other destruction oriented cybercrime focus. If you remember, Anonymous, and other related groups were targeting companies they fundamentally disagreed with on ideology. Their response was to shut these companies down with denial of service (DDOS) attacks, demanding a change in policy or activity. They proved that large companies were defenseless against their attacks. They would announce, "We'll shut you down tomorrow if you don't respond." Then, that next day they would do it. They didn't need a surprise attack because their DDOS attacks were over-powering and successful. Cyberwarfare takes this a step further.

Wall Street Journal reports tell us that ISIS has launched some of the most effective, global influence campaigns in history using online tools like Facebook and websites.

Young people have been converted, recruited, and indoctrinated online to the point of selling everything they own to move and join the cause. On the other side of their conversion, we hear stories of rape, torture, and human trafficking. But still, people continue to respond to the cause, even to the point of carrying out suicide missions with bombs strapped to their bodies.

We've been at war with cybercrime for at least the past fifteen years. Governments have been in a larger scale information stealing war as long as they've been around. But ISIS, and other more recent battles, have opened the door to a new kind of war: the traditional ground battle, waged online.

The line is fuzzy. Was the Sony Pictures hack an act of war carried out by those in North Korea? Or was it more like a major act of vandalism by some other group? Even security experts disagree on this topic. No one knows. But the recent SWIFT attack certainly adds credibility to the North Korea theory.

What about StuxNet? Did Israel and the US build this software to take down a nuclear warfare effort, or was it done by hackers looking to stop something they didn't like. No one has raised their hand. Most security experts agree, this was a government sponsored effort involving the US and Israel.

Getting Ready for Cyberbattles

Cyber Command is the U.S. military counterpart to the NSA Over the past six years, this group has been growing and preparing, largely focused on Russia, China, Iran, and North Korea.

According to news reports, Cyber Command is where most cyberattacks originate. ISIS has not been a target, until recently. In an April, 2016 report, we are told that the US is putting their focus on the Islamic State, alongside our more traditional weapons.

Working in cooperation with Germany, England, and France, this effort was established to stop, or slow the Islamic State as they work to spread their propaganda, attract new members, and pass on orders from their commanders. Little is known about this campaign, its successes, or its failures. It claims to use secret weapons, and is called the newest warfare campaign. The hope is that new recruits will think twice about joining as they realize just how serious the US and its allies are about stopping those who would attack through the Internet.

Examples Close to Home

Kosovo War Example

On May 7, 1999, NATO jets bombed the Chinese embassy in Belgrade. At that time, they were supporting the Yugoslav army. 12 hours later, the Chinese Red Hacker Alliance retaliated by launching thousands of cyberattacks against US government websites.

Operation Cast Lead Example

In 2006, Israel launched *Operation Cast Lead*, an attack on the Palestine National Authority. These battles included cyberattacks against government websites, involving both nation-state (government) and non-state actors.

The Tulip Revolution II

December, 2009 – April, 2010: Kazakhstan intelligence units broke into Journalist Gennady Pavlyuk's email to obtain business intellectual capital. Then, with data in hand, they lured him to Kazakhstan under the pretense of meeting angel investors. Pavlyuk was assassinated upon arrival, which resulted in a series of attacks on opposition websites.

StuxNet

I've already covered this one in the first threat; software. Stuxnet is a great example of the power software holds to destroy physical plant and infrastructure. It's estimated that this one software program took over 15 man-years to develop. The end result was stealthy and powerful, setting Iranian nuclear development efforts back by at least 2 years.

Who's at Risk?

Everyone is affected when a war breaks out. If it's overseas, it might be the economy, a loved one, or even deployment.

When cyberwarfare ensues, the collateral damage can be devastating. In the US, we rarely see large scale attacks on the lives of private citizens, although it does apparently happen. Most of our attacks are small, (but still devastating,) acts of terrorism.

But with groups like ISIS, (A war on terrorism), the public is always the target. As cyberwarfare efforts grow around the world, we can expect wars to become more damaging. The US in particular, has been insulated by vast oceans since its founding years ago.

The Internet knows no boundaries, and as nations and terrorist groups decide to attack, it is likely they'll use computers to knock out critical infrastructure, affecting larger groups of people.

Steps You Can Take to Reduce Your Exposure

You may have guessed this already, but there's not much you can do to stop or avoid a war. However, there are things you can do to avoid being part of the collateral damage.

The weapons of destruction are generally the same. Malware, such as ransomware, bots, etc. Don't underestimate these. The intent is different. Traditional hackers are looking for new ways to make money. They steal your data, hope you'll continue to create new revenue opportunities, and sell your stuff on the black market.

In war, the goal is destruction. ISIS funds their war with drug money, human trafficking, and other illegal activities. But chances are, your company is not that interesting to them. Guard yourself from malware, maintain a solid backup and recovery strategy, and hope that the government is watching the right things, (but assume they are not).

As we move into Part II, I'll be showing you the one, big

mistake, which is foundational to just about every breach. This is the place to start, and it is your best chance of surviving the growing threats that accompany the benefits of the Digitalization Megatrend.

Part Two

THE ONE BIG MISTAKE

THERE ARE MANY CONTRIBUTORS, BUT THIS ONE BIG MISTAKE IS FOUNDATIONAL TO SO MANY DISASTERS – BOTH PHYSICAL AND DIGITAL. FIX THIS ONE THING, AND 80% OF THE PROBLEM GOES AWAY!

CHAPTER ELEVEN

How Secure is Your House?

Through centuries of war and criminal activity, society has understood physical security. But you might be surprised when you see what actually secures your house, and even more surprised to find out what really secures your data.

Just a couple of weeks ago, I got the news that my neighbor's home had been robbed. Another neighbor noticed a white sedan in their driveway, with the garage door open, but assumed it was a contractor or cleaning service. It was the middle of the day. With both parents at work, and the kids in school, the house was an easy target.

Somehow, these crooks knew the house was empty. Later we learned that this same sedan had been canvassing the neighborhood, probably observing the habits of the houses around us, including our home.

These intruders made their way to the back of my neighbor's house, hidden by thick, wooded landscape, and used a ladder to access an upstairs window. From there, they made their way through the house, opened the garage, and began loading electronics, jewelry, and anything that looked like an easy pawn shop item into the back of their car.

My neighbors were horrified. Our neighborhood has never experienced this type of criminal activity in the past 20 years of its existence. We're out in the country, away from big city crime, and next to a very conservative, low-crime town. The police station sits right across the street from our neighborhood entry. How could something like this happen?

It Gets Worse: The Robberies Continued

One break-in is enough to put the entire neighborhood on high-alert. But this wasn't an isolated incident! Over the next two weeks, four more homes were hit, and several strange cars were spotted sitting in cul-de-sacs. All daytime hits, these criminals were targeting homes with working parents and kids in school. What were they after? Stuff that's easy to pawn or sell online.

One neighbor managed to catch a possible criminal on camera, wandering through their backyard. But no arrests were made.

The police began regular patrols, but even with law enforcement patrolling, the perpetrators continued their crime spree. Will it happen again? What's to stop them? Why is it so easy for criminals to steal, even in the presence of the police?

What Makes Something Secure?

Is your home safe from this type of thing? The truth is, any home can be invaded, but all four of these homes were missing the most important elements of security. They were making the one big mistake mentioned at the start of this book.

I am hopeful that our home won't be hit. I also know we are not making this one mistake. It doesn't mean that our home is impenetrable, but it does greatly decrease the likelihood of our home being hit. Like the guy trying to outrun a bear, if he can just outrun his friend, he'll be safe. His friend on the other hand…well, he's in trouble. The same is true with our home. They'll go next door if they know we've thought about this.

So what is it that makes a home secure?

Society as a Whole Misunderstands Risk and Security: Setting Us Up for Failure

This big mistake is getting bigger. Not only are homes being broken into, but in addition, computers are being hit every day. Their security safeguards are no match for hackers when this one principle is violated.

Things are getting worse. This has been a violent year in the news. Mass shootings have been reported around the US. Shootings in churches and schools, and even random acts of killing on city streets are becoming more and more frequent. Just recently, twelve police officers were shot in Dallas, Texas by a rooftop sniper. Five died in the line of duty!

It doesn't make sense. Some are terrorist driven, while others are just crazy, angry people. But we can't stop these attacks, at least not easily. In most cases, these people are not open to reason or negotiation. They have a cause, it's violent, it's sick, and unless stopped, they'll carry it out regardless of the cost. You can't negotiate with people like this.

But again, this one principle of security greatly reduces the likelihood of disaster when applied correctly. When left out, criminals, terrorist, and crazy people have a field day. We all pay the price. What is this important aspect of securing both physical and digital assets, that our society seems to be missing?

The Principle of The House

My home isn't bulletproof, but it is pretty safe. Why? Have you ever taken time to think about what it is that actually makes something secure? Rather than looking at budgets and products, think about the theory behind keeping something safe.

As I travel around the world speaking to business leaders, I use a house because it's easy to see. We all live in houses and most of us feel a sense of safety in our home. I hope you do. But let's evaluate just how safe your home really is.

What secures your home? If you were to start outlining your home security strategy, you might come up with a list that looks like this:

Doors	Alarm	Dogs
Windows	Motion Detection	Gun
Locks	Monitoring	Police
Fence	Crime Watch	Insurance

You might have some or all of these things, but hopefully you've invested in the ones that matter most, based on where you live. Security has to take into account your location, your assets, and your relationships.

In general, this list above is what people rely on to protect their homes. But when you look deeper into security, you'll quickly see that these things are not what primarily secure your house. You've been told that they do, you've spent money on them, you've placed your trust in them, but you've been somewhat led astray.

Locks, Alarms, and Safes Don't Secure Your Home. So What Does?

There's actually a system at work behind these *security controls*. It's a system that flows from left to right, comprised of PROTECTION, DETECTION, and RESPONSE.

All three are required for a security program to work. It must be well-timed, and it must flow in sequence, left to right. If it doesn't, your security plan will fail when put to the test.

All Are Necessary, But One is Paramount

When I speak on this subject, it's always an eye-opening experience. Perhaps you've never thought about this sequence, but this is how security works. The next question you must answer is, "Which of these columns is most important?" All three are necessary, but one must be nearly perfect. It must have the right components, and they must be tested. Then there's a second level of importance, and finally the third. So all three are needed, but there is a definite order of importance and timing to make it all work.

If I were speaking to you in a live session, I would be asking for a raise of hands. Which of the three do you think it is? If you're the person responsible for security in your organization, my guess is you know the answer (although many CISOs have guessed wrongly). What about the end-users in your company, the ones that actually create and use this data. Do they know? Does the average small business owner know? The answer is "No." Having presented these truths for the past 15 years to groups all over the world, I can tell you that most people choose the wrong column. At best, we get a split vote. But in many cases, 90% will vote incorrectly.

It's what we've been told, mostly by security sales people and manufacturers. The vote usually swings to the left, landing on PROTECTION. Perhaps the early firewall companies started this with firewall marketing claims, stating their product was impenetrable. Prior to the Internet, I think most of us understood. Somehow the thinking has changed with computers. If you guessed correctly, you guessed DETECTION. RESPONSE is a close second, and PROTECTION comes in third. It's exactly opposite of how most people vote. Let's take a look at why.

Understanding the Most Important Column in Security

Look at your home. Many years ago, men tried protecting their cities with castle walls. It failed. Tunnels were built, doors were burned, and men sacrificed their lives to scale long ladders, with a plan of eventually overwhelming the fortress.

Prisons and war camps are the same. People continue to break out through tunnels and other ruses that baffle those responsible for securing the perimeter.

Today, we don't live in castles. We buy alarms. I don't think anyone would argue that their house can't be broken into. Take away the detection, and I can get into your home in a few minutes. Whether it's the fear of being seen, or perhaps being hit by someone's aggressive response plan, criminals are looking for targets that allow them to go undetected. They know they can get in if there's little to no detection.

The homes hit in my neighborhood were no exception. Invaders came through the back windows, knowing the home was empty. In this case, all five neighbors failed to have alarm systems armed and ready on the windows that were compromised. These criminals took their time, loaded their car, and drove off in broad daylight. They did it five times because they had done their research, and believed they could remain undetected.

The bank proves this every day. Go into any local branch, and you'll observe that the doors are open for day time business. If you were to make your way to the back, you would find that the vault is open too. Bankers need access, so it's sitting there accessible. So what protects the money? Detection and response.

Understanding Response

The second most important column is the response column. But not just any response. It must be a real-time response. By real time, we mean fast enough to counteract the crime. At the bank, that might be under an hour. In computer time, it's nearly instantaneous. Home invasions are slower, but still require a timely response. Mass shootings, as I've already stated, only last for 11 minutes before they're over. Immediate detection, and disabling response must be present and onsite, or it won't work.

The Principle of The Cloud

Now let's look at data security. How are most computers protected: passwords, firewalls, and encryption. Remember, most businesses are small businesses, which lack the sophisticated security strategies employed by banks and the military. Notice that they all fall in column one. They all claim to keep people out.

If physical security requires all three, but depends on column two, data should be the same. It's just faster. In fact, it needs to be much more robust – quicker, stronger detection. Since data is invisible, you can't expect to detect the crime without special detection tools.

Your home may be in a safe neighborhood, but regardless of

where you plug in, your computer is not. It's connected to the debauched people I listed earlier; people who want your money, your children, and your spouse, and will do just about anything to get it, including killing you. Yet, because you work on your computer in a safe building, or in a safe business park, the thought is, "We're safe." It's deceptive, isn't it?

As a result, if you were to Google some statistics like: "*What percentage of computers are infected with malware?*", or "*How long can a computer sit, unprotected by antivirus software, and not be hit?*" You would come up with some scary statistics. One sound bite from the Wall Street Journal stated that over 250,000 computers are infected by malware every day. That's pretty sobering. At that rate, it won't take long to infect every computer on the planet. Obviously, this takes into consideration computers that are being infected, cleaned, and re-infected.

Failed Security Strategies

My neighbors are all installing alarms and cameras this week. In fact, we've added a few cameras to our property just to beef up security in the heat of the threat.

Our home was well protected because, with nine people living there (2 parents and 7 kids), it's rare that our home is empty. We also have three, large German Shepherds roaming our property at all times. They are well trained and look scary. Two signs greet people at the front of our driveway. One warns people of the dogs; the other advertises our alarm monitoring company. Between people, cameras, and alarms, we have detection pretty well covered.

But there's still a breakdown in many homes. Look at your home for a minute and image the following scenario. It's late at night when you and your spouse are abruptly awakened by your alarm. It's blaring loudly as you scramble to your feet. Just a week ago, after reading my book, you installed a new alarm. Great!

You've also taken extra steps to connect with an alarm monitoring company featuring cellular connection, so the signal is sent and received. Fifteen seconds later, your phone rings. It's the alarm company, calling to see if you're okay. At that moment, you hear the sound of footsteps charging up the stairs toward your bedroom. Your kids are in their rooms down the hall. Now what happens?

The alarm might scare the average criminal, but not all. What's your response plan? Remember, response must be real time. The last time our alarm went off, it was the middle of the night. The police dispatch said it would be twenty minutes before the police officers could arrive. Even with the police station across the street, it was still a 20 minute wait. When this happens, and there's no backup plan, security fails. You might take the call from your alarm company, but what will you do to stop whatever threat might be advancing toward you and your family?

If my neighbors are at work, and the alarm goes off, they'll know they've been hit. But unless another neighbor runs over there, prepared to stop the intruders, assets will still be stolen. If the intruders happen to run into you unexpectedly, the crime is likely to escalate. What's your response plan now?

In the case of the mass shootings, detection is almost immediate, but often after the shooting has already started. As I've stated, the average active shooter incident is an eleven minute ordeal. SWAT can't respond that fast. So unless there are armed people onsite when it happens, the security plan will fail. This is the problem with most of the gun control talk out there. Few understand that law enforcement cannot stop an incident in progress unless they are already there. Their job does not involve preventative detection.

In a recent, ten week citizen's police academy program, our local police chief made it clear that they need our help. They can't defend the city proactively. They encouraged us to be trained and ready in the event of a break in or attack.

When it comes to data protection, the same is true. It happens so fast that human detection is almost meaningless. When a small business owner looks around and doesn't see computer problems, they can't make the assumption that all is OK. By the time they detect an issue, it will be too late. The average detection takes months, and often more than a year. TJ Maxx took about three years. Home Depot and Target found out 3 to 4 months after their 2015 breaches. JP Morgan was the same.

Real time detection and response are necessary if you are going to secure anything.

What Does Good Data Security Look Like?

Good security happens when all nine boxes in the chart below converge into one seamless program. It won't be completely technical, and it won't be impenetrable. But it will take you from a false sense of security to a detection strategy, followed by real-time response. This is a program that will allow you to stop most of the threats that come your way.

	Protection	**Detection**	**Response**
Admin			DR Plan
Technical	Firewall		
Physical		Guard	

I call this the *Coverage Model*. Remember, the three columns are PROTECTION, DETECTION, and RESPONSE. In the rows underneath their headings, you'll see three layers: *Administrative, Technical,* and *Physical.*

☐ **Protection.** Like in the house, these controls keep things out. Firewalls, passwords, and encryption are all forms of proactive protection, designed to keep unauthorized users away from your data.

- ☐ **Detection.** At this point in the model, something has broken through your protective barrier. The faster you can detect this breach, the better. Security technology companies are working hard to build this functionality into their products. Unfortunately, many of the better products are unaffordable for smaller businesses. However, IT services companies are now making these services available through third party providers at a reasonable price. Better services include a team of security analysts watching online to see if a breach occurs.

- ☐ **Response.** Once detected, time is short. A real time response will automatically block suspicious traffic, quarantining it for further inspection. It will also alert security experts who understand the anatomy of an attack, and who can respond properly, while also maintaining the necessary chain of custody to track down the perpetrators.

- ☐ **Administrative.** The first row in the model refers to security at the end-user level. Controls like sign-in logs, security policies, and user awareness training would all fall under this category, divided across the areas of protection, detection, and response.

- ☐ **Technical**. The second row in our model lists the technology: firewalls, intrusion detection appliances, and other computerized security devices. While in the physical world, a human being may be able to see something and respond to it. On the other hand, data is fast and invisible. The hacker is stealthy, and invisible apart from specialized detection and response technology.

- ☐ **Physical**. This row deals with the actual physical rooms and facilities where data, systems, and networks are housed. Companies will spend enormous sums of money on physical security to keep unauthorized personnel out of the computer room, only to leave the data-doors wide open on the network side. Both are needed. Smaller businesses may put their data servers in a back closet with little or no physical security. This is a mistake. Computer theft can potentially confiscate all of your data in one short moment, if not backed up to the cloud, or some offsite server. Once a hacker has your computer, encryption won't keep them from taking your data, (including your smartphone and tablet).

Creating a Safe Computing Environment

Gartner Group estimates that about 80% of a company's security budget is spent on column one. But as we've seen here, the first layer doesn't have to be bulletproof. Like a house, pretty good security, (considering the value of the assets inside), works. The bank will have stronger column one controls, such as a very sophisticated safe. The house will have doors and windows that are mostly designed for energy efficiency, not asset protection.

In the case of the homes in my neighborhood, detection is needed. But the likelihood of a breach, until last week, was pretty low. The homes that had a visible level of detection were left alone. Those that didn't were hit.

In the bank, people are willing to take a bigger risk for a bigger payoff. In this case, column one is pretty strong at night. But it can still be broken. Safe manufactures readily admit that their safes can be compromised. In fact, the safe's rating system indicates just how long it will hold up to a torch and tools. But you can be sure the bank has a timed response plan once that alarm goes off. The police will be there before the crook breaks into the safe.

Computer security depends a lot on the people creating and using the data. Most data breaches involve mistakes made by those who create and use data. A laptop left in the airport, a phone sold before deleting its contents, or an email opened that contains malware.

In Part III, I'll give you seven mindsets that, if instilled in the end-users' minds, will help move your company closer to detection, with a lower likelihood of making a mistake.

Part Three

A NEW MINDSET

DATA SECURITY IS NOT A TECHNICAL PROBLEM; IT'S A PEOPLE PROBLEM. ESTABLISH A CULTURE OF DATA SECURITY IN YOUR BUSINESS. IT STARTS WITH BUILDING NEW MINDSETS AND RETHINKING THE VALUE OF THE DATA WE CREATE AND USE EVERY DAY TO CONDUCT BUSINESS

CHAPTER TWELVE

Mindset One: Data is Money

Networks and computers are not worth much when compared to your company data or personal wealth. A wrong focus can put everything at risk. Your phone is not just a phone. It's a storage device, capable of holding or accessing just about everything you value.

By now you know full well, digital money is not only about cybercurrencies or the data that makes up your bank account. It is also high-value data of any kind. Data in today's economy is one of your company's most valuable assets. Right or wrong, in many cases, it's regarded as more important than even the people sitting around you.

Years ago, a news report from London appeared in The Wall Street Journal. The writer went on to describe an office worker who was responsible for losing over $1,000,000 USD in data. The data had been written to a DVD and passed on to the appropriate department through their interoffice mail system. When it didn't arrive as expected, the company management went ballistic. What happened?

The reporter's perspective was on the money. This office worker wasn't thinking about the value of the data. His attention was on the inexpensive media. A cheap, replaceable DVD didn't need any special oversight. The reporter went on to ask the all-important question, "Would this office worker have placed this much cash in an interoffice envelope?" The answer of course is "No."

Large amounts of money are moved every day in business. Some money is wired, some transported by armored car. No one puts large sums of cash in the hands of the interoffice mail delivery guy.

Was it stolen, or just misplaced? We'll never know. But my guess is, that office worker either lost his job or his reputation... probably both.

The Typical Mindset: The Technology Mindset

The technology mindset plagues almost every company I work with. Here are some of the signs that people around you are thinking *Technology*, and not, *Assets*:

☐ IT is responsible for security, while executive management is disengaged.

☐ The company's user awareness program is either sparse or nonexistent.

☐ Security upgrades are completely based on budget, not an evaluation of impact vs. likelihood.

☐ Employees are more concerned about losing their laptop or phone than they are about the data on that device.

☐ Employees are not educated about the value of the data on their computing devices.

☐ The hardware is insured, but the data is not.

☐ The computer room is locked, (physical security), but online security is weak.

☐ Data security is not assessed on a regular basis. There is no impact vs. likelihood graph.

☐ The company is quick to retrieve hardware during an employee's exit interview, but no attention is given to ensuring that data is not leaving with that person. Online accounts may also remain active long after their departure.

The Asset Mindset Defined: Data is Money

Every day, phones and laptops are misplaced, left unguarded in coffee shops, and tossed around as though they were the AT&T phones of the seventies. They're not.

I often spend afternoons working in our local Starbucks. I can't tell you how many times I've see people leave their phones and laptops, open to the public eye, and unguarded, to visit the restroom.

The Asset Mindset is a mindset that thinks about the value of data. Data is money. It's *digital money*. Consider the value of data.

☐ **Your bank account is just a bunch of data**. A screen on your computer says that you have $500,000 in an investment. You and I know that your bank does not have $500,000 sitting in the vault with your name on it. It's just data on a ledger.

☐ **Personal Data**. Your personal data defines much of who you are to the government, your bankers, your employer, and your doctors. Anyone can claim to be you if they have the right data. That means they can take out loans, purchase expensive equipment, make decisions on your behalf, and instruct others to carry out tasks using your authority. With the right credentials, they can even command groups of people you have authority over.

☐ **Your online profiles and social media**. While you might not think of Facebook data as money, the aggregation of data, and access to profiles such as your Facebook account, control your online reputation. False data posted to an account, or the revelation of data you don't want exposed, can affect your employment, friendships, and family/marriage relationships. A good name is critical in all aspects of business today.

☐ **Health data**. EMR has put your entire health history online. Employers are likely to be influenced by health issues you're not required to disclose. Friendships can also be affected. And fraudulent purchases made using your health record information could quickly overload you with debts you cannot pay. Try getting these cleared and you might be surprised by how hard it is to prove you didn't do it. Once your data is stolen, it's actually very hard to prove that you are you!

Adopting the Right Mindset: The Asset Mindset

Data is money. The sooner your team understands the value of data, the safer your data will be. Every moment of every day, people all around you are creating, using, transmitting, and deleting data. Some of that data is worth a fortune. The right data has the power to put you out of business if accidentally deleted, corrupted, suddenly made inaccessible, or somehow misused.

Start building an Asset Mindset. Forget about the product and focus on the assets...your digital assets. The data on your laptop may not mean much to you, but to your company it might mean everything. Begin adopting this mindset by securing all of your computing devices:

Guard Your Computer

☐ Use computer locks on your desks in the office. Lock your office door if you have one.

☐ Don't leave computers and phones in public places, especially high traffic areas like Starbucks, lobbies, airports, etc. Save your seat with a jacket or book, and take your electronics to the restroom if you have to get up.

☐ Laptops left in cars are easy prey. Take them with you.

☐ Don't stand in crowded locations such as bus stops or subway stations, glued to your iPhone. Reports of grab-n-dash crimes continue to grow, so be alert. People won't generally steal from someone who appears to be on the alert.

☐ Record your serial numbers with local law enforcement sites so that these devices cannot be pawned. One easy way to capture this data is to photograph using something like

Evernote, keeping your serial numbers in a backed-up cloud file.

Maintain Your Software

☐ All computers should have some type of antivirus software on them. Different manufacturers recommend different things (e.g. Apple vs. Microsoft). Steer clear of free antivirus solutions.

☐ All software has bugs, and lots of them! Software updates should be applied. Some recommend using auto updates, but I prefer to wait a day. If the patch is good, it will be there tomorrow. If the developer finds a problem, it will be replaced. Antivirus updates are critical and should be applied immediately and automatically.

☐ Phone apps are updated frequently. Some are functionality updates, but most address bugs. Hackers exploit bugs to gain access, so stay on top of app updates on your phone. Phone OS updates take longer to load, and can sometimes be a burden. Make time to install these updates.

Use Firewalls – Software and Hardware

☐ All company networks should be protected by UTM (Universal Threat Management) firewalls. In most cases (other than very small micro businesses), you will want someone monitoring your firewall 24/7. This means they are watching for alerts on a continuous basis. Periodic firewall administration is no longer enough. Most firewalls have additional detection capabilities built in. Use them!

☐ Enable your computer's software firewall. This software restricts other computers from connecting directly to yours without explicit permission. In cases where a connection is required, (such as using Airdrop on a Mac), the user can authorize that connection even while the software firewall is running. Too many people turn these off when they run into access problems with printers and network functions.

☐ In larger businesses, departments with more sensitive data should be segmented using firewalls between departmental networks. Even small businesses can do this today using smaller, affordable firewalls with multiple network ports. As IoT catches on, this will become even more critical. Internet facing applications should sit on a separate segment, usually referred to as the DMZ.

Back Up Constantly, in Multiple Places

☐ Back up all data using your computer manufacturer's recommended tools. Many of the files you need may not be visible, or where you expect them to be, (Note: experts estimate that over 77% of backup restores fail, and data is lost.)

☐ The Cloud is a popular tool for backing up data. Companies like Google have made this very affordable. However, you can't restore an entire computer from the cloud; it's too slow. Use cloud backup as a secondary backup in case of a disaster.

☐ Use local backups on all mobile and desktop systems. I recommend a locally attached NAS (Network Attached Storage) that has the ability to back itself up to the cloud.

☐ Use continuous backup. Especially when working on anything mission critical. You can't afford to a lose an entire day's work.

☐ Protect yourself against ransomware. Your best defense against this rapidly growing attack is detection and response. In the event that your perimeter does not detect this intrusion in time, you will want a clean backup! The alternative is either data loss or paying the piper.

- ☐ Remember, all hardware will fail at some point. Don't look to your backup solution as the place to save money.

Use Encrypted Connections and Watch Out for Rogue Access Points (AP)

- ☐ Your office network should be set up to use the latest encryption algorithms. A separate segment should be set up for guest users.

- ☐ If your employees work from home, you should be providing them with instructions to encrypt their home networks before using them for business. Encrypted home networks should also be specified in your security policy.

- ☐ The public networks we all use are not safe. However, your employees are going to use them. In this case, users are relying on personal firewall software on their computers. Make sure they understand how to use them.

- ☐ Be vigilant to know what network you should be connecting to. Rogue APs are easily set up to lure unsuspecting users. This is often referred to as a man-in-the-middle attack, and will lead to data theft. Ask the store manager if you're not sure.

Encrypt Your Hard Drive

- ☐ An encrypted hard drive puts one more obstacle in front of the hacker. Both your phone and laptop should be encrypted. Your phone should be setup to erase itself after ten attempts at the password. Keep your encryption password somewhere safe and out of reach.

Maintain a Password Vault

- ☐ If you are like most people, you have too many accounts to remember a unique password for each. A password vault is essential if you're going to rely on passwords to protect your data.

☐ Use strong passwords. A good software vault application will build the passwords for you and rate their security level. This is far better than trying to think up something no one will guess.

☐ Use different passwords for different accounts. If one gets compromised, the others will still be safe.

☐ Don't leave your password vault sitting open at the local coffee shop. And remember to back it up too.

Watch Out for Phishing and Other Scams

☐ Email phishing is the most likely place for an attack to take place. Guard your inbox, and don't open anything suspicious.

☐ Don't assume you can't be infected by botware without clicking. New exploits do not require you to click anything. Use spam filtering, sandbox technology at the perimeter, and watch what you click on.

☐ Avoid any attachments that might be executable files. This includes *.zip, *.doxm, *.exe, *.dmg etc. Unless you know someone has legitimately sent this file to you, delete it immediately. Knowing the sender is not enough. It's easy for hackers to send mail that looks like it came from a co-worker or friend.

☐ If asked in an email to do something out of the ordinary, or that may be highly sensitive (such as updating banking information), it's best to call the person rather than blindly carrying out the request.

Browse Wisely

☐ When browsing, use a reputable browser such as Chrome or Firefox. If you notice your search engine is reverting from Google, Yahoo, or whatever you normally use, stop. Rogue applications sometimes get downloaded while working on something legitimate, and will take over your system. This is a system hijacking situation. You may need to get professional assistance to clean things up.

☐ Don't look too hard for the best price. It's easy to set up a fraudulent website. If you don't know who you're buying from, don't expect them to be trustworthy.

☐ Use PayPal or your credit card when shopping online. Do not use debit cards. Debit cards, if compromised, can be used to withdraw money from your account. In most cases, credit card purchases are protected by the card issuer, but check the terms of the card you are using.

☐ Beware of unwanted downloads. Read the websites and pop-ups before taking action. Free tools that do things like convert YouTube to MP3 may be needed, but watch out for sites that download unwanted plugins as part of the download.

☐ Block pop-ups. You can then allow the ones you really want when your browser detects them.

Be Cloud Savvy

The cloud is here. Most enterprise businesses have about half of their applications in the cloud. 80% of small businesses will move to the cloud over the next few years. It is important that you become knowledgeable regarding cloud computing, how it works, and where to be cautious.

Is it safe? Many have asked me if cloud computing is risky. After all, you are putting your data on someone else's network. My opinion is that in most cases, it's good. Reputable cloud providers are serving major companies with serious data. That tells me they have a big investment in security. Much bigger that most readers of this book will have.

- ☐ Before contracting with a cloud company, be sure to read the documentation. Who owns your data? If the court subpoena's your data, what will that company do?

- ☐ What happens if the cloud company goes out of business? What happens to your data then? If your CRM, (Customer Relationship Management), hosting company closes their doors, will you lose your data?

- ☐ Where is your data located? India's laws differ from US laws, etc. Do you know who's laws your data falls under?

- ☐ Be aware of cost structures. What happens as your data volume grows?

- ☐ Is your cloud provider secure? Who has access to your data, and is it stored in an encrypted format? Look for a reputable company. Your cloud services can't come from a low-cost provider. Remember, they are holding your *digital money*.

ACTION ITEMS TO SECURE YOUR ASSETS

- ✓ Record all device serial numbers on your local law enforcement website to prevent thieves from pawning stolen electronics.
- ✓ Enable auto updates on all antivirus software.
- ✓ Schedule regular times to update other software and phone apps.
- ✓ Turn on firewalls on all devices. Contract with a security operations center, (SOC), to watch over your business-class UTM firewall and other security devices.
- ✓ Move all Internet-facing apps to a DMZ, as well as guest access networks.

✓ Set all systems to be continuously backed up locally. Set local backups to back up to a cloud service such as Amazon.
✓ Encrypt all networks and hard drives.
✓ Purchase and maintain a password vault. Change all passwords, using unique passwords on each account.
✓ Turn on your browser pop-up blocker – and make sure your browser is directing you to a reputable search engine such as Google or Yahoo.
✓ Check out your cloud provider. Make sure you are using someone reputable to hold your most important assets.

Getting Your Company Focused on Assets

Your data may be your most valuable assets. Compromised companies often go out of business once a breach is disclosed. Larger companies are sure to take a hit on company valuation.

To get your company thinking about this the right way, start with data classification. Security policies don't actually secure anything, but they do limit liability and give guidance to the creation, usage, and storage of data. Start here:

Classify Your Data

☐ *Public*: No local (business), national, or international restriction on access. Open to the public.

☐ *Internal Only*: Data that should only be viewed by employees of the company, or by those with special approval from the appropriate, company officers.

☐ *Restricted Access*: Data that should only be seen by approved employees or related business associates.

☐ *Top Secret*: This level may have some overlap with Restricted Access, but the term *Top Secret* reminds those with access that this level of privilege is extremely limited. Documents might include payroll, income statements, or product formulas regarded as the company's intellectual property.

Purposeful Access Control

Once data is classified, user access should be controlled on a need to know basis. Data should be stored centrally using internal, external, or hybrid cloud technologies to keep users from maintaining too much company data on their local systems.

Your company will need a process to maintain access control restrictions through the lifecycle of any given employee. As job functions change, so should access privileges.

User Awareness Training and Accountability

Employee education on the value of data, current trends in hacker activities, and scams will help reduce the likelihood of being lured into giving up data and access through clever social engineering schemes.

Security policies should be updated, distributed, and read. In the event of a breach or compliance violation, you should have a record of when your employees were asked to read the policy, and a signature verifying that they have actually read it. Policies should cover aspects of data including usage, access, transmission, handling, storage, and deletion/archival.

Keep in mind that policies which are not enforced are interpreted by the court as a recommendation. In other words, if you don't consistently enforce a policy, you may not be able to enforce it at all. At this point, your liability may no longer be limited.

CHAPTER THIRTEEN

Mindset Two: Compliance is Not Security

> Compliance is the law; but don't confuse it with security. Compliance is the bureaucracy that creeps in when companies don't secure their data. The more you allow criminals to access your data, the more the government will feel the need to impose expensive laws that don't always help you.

Last year I was invited to speak to doctors and hospital administrators at a healthcare conference. The conference meeting planners had invited me to attend other sessions throughout the week, so I took them up on their generous offer.

Just about every session I attended that had anything to do with data security seemed to focus on HIPAA. When it was my turn to speak, I started by asking the audience to forget about HIPAA for just one hour. The response was predictable. I could tell immediately that my audience was confused. After all, anyone in healthcare knows that HIPAA sets the standards for security in the healthcare industry.

In another incident, a major grocery chain, that was reportedly PCI compliant, was breached. The incident resulted in the exposure of millions of credit card numbers. Once reported, that company was told they were no longer considered compliant. The point here is that a company can be said to be compliant, but not actually be. Or, they may actually be compliant, but still be vulnerable. Security and compliance are not the same thing.

My healthcare talk was specifically about securing digital assets, not HIPAA or any other compliance requirement. The two are vastly different.

The Traditional Mindset: Compliance Equals Security

Compliance laws have our attention. If you're not careful, it's easy to place all of your focus on compliance, rather than thinking through the security of your data. Don't let the government determine whether or not your data is safe. If it's compromised, they are not going to insure it for you. Your data is your responsibility. Following are some signs that your company is thinking too hard about compliance.

☐ When asked about security, you respond by talking about your compliance program.

☐ When there's a security discussion, or an update presented at your board meeting, the answer starts with the status of compliance.

☐ The only steps you've taken to secure data are those specified by the compliance regulations that govern your business.

☐ In the past year, your company has not assessed risk other than what is required by compliance.

☐ You think that port scanning your network for HIPAA or PCI is the same thing as a risk assessment.

☐ You would rather pay the fine than comply with compliance standards. Remember, compliance is necessary, it's just not security.

The Security, (Not Compliance), Mindset Defined: Compliance Does Not Secure Data

Your risk is measured on the Impact vs. Likelihood graph. The likelihood of a breach is where you want to focus. If you have the right mindset, you are more concerned with where your data is, who has access to it, and how likely it is that you will suffer some sort of breach or unexpected security event in the next twelve to eighteen months.

Because hackers are coming up with new attacks all the time, the assessment process must be ongoing, and the detection element of your security must be real-time. Consider the differences:

☐ Compliance laws are more focused on paperwork than detection. Real security happens when your people and systems are set up to detect unauthorized access or usage of your data.

☐ Compliance assessments often rely on scanning ports and reviewing policies. True security watches data for activities symptomatic of a breach or misuse. A response program stands poised to react.

☐ Compliance relies on governments to understand the risks you face in business. True security looks to experienced, security professionals that evaluate your data, your industry, your current business climate, and your company's specific risks, which will often differ from other like companies.

☐ Security and hackers are fast moving targets. New things are popping up every day. Government standards and policies take years to develop, and the alignment of numerous people to make even miniscule changes. The likelihood of any compliance directive being up-to-date and relevant, is small to say the least.

Adopting the Right Mindset: The Security with Regard for Compliance Mindset

First, don't get me wrong, I am not for one minute telling you to avoid HIPAA or any other law regarding computers or security. There are some serious fines that could put you out of business if you do!

However, compliance is hurting us from a security standpoint. When companies focus solely on compliance, allocate lots of money to it, and check off all the right boxes, they often think they're good. It's a misconception.

There are many regulations. I've named a few. Some of the regulations make sense, while many of them don't. Expect lots of paperwork, and lots of reporting, but not a lot of detection/response in these laws. If you look at HIPAA for instance, you will see laws regarding the privacy of patient data. Some of that is good. On the other hand, there is little to prevent a hacker from gaining access to that data. And the amount of work required for small clinics to maintain HIPAA requirements is significant. In fact, as compliance regulations continue to grow, (and they probably will), I wonder who will be able to afford them.

Start building the mindset, "We need to be compliant, but let's also be secure." Remember, if everyone is more secure, there will be less compliance imposed on your business. Compliance is the bureaucracy government imposes when things are in disarray. It's their way of saying, "We're doing something about this." The truth is, they are making it more expensive for companies like yours to conduct business. You can help yourself and all companies by establishing some of the following practices in your own business.

Work Towards Compliance

☐ Compliance is the law. Make sure you are up-to-date on what the law requires for your specific data and line of work. Encourage your representatives to vote "No" to additional compliance laws, unless you are sure the proposed changes really will help secure data.

☐ Contract with local security firms to provide a gap analysis to determine where you fall short. Consider letting a qualified technology company guide you through the process.

☐ Have a compliance officer on your team, (contracted or full time), if you have serious compliance requirements imposed on your business. This role should be separate from that of securing data.

☐ Be prepared for an audit. Expect compliance laws to grow in their complexity, cost, and accountability.

Assess Your Actual Risk on a Regular Basis

☐ Assess your risk by building the Impact vs. Likelihood graph for your own business. This should be updated quarterly.

☐ Hire outside, qualified experts to perform your risk assessments. Don't settle for pen-testing or port scanning. Find a provider that understands how to detect symptoms of intrusion, and who knows what technology should be used to detect and respond in real time. Note: it is not necessary to work with a different company than the one you hire to monitor security. In my opinion, it is better to have the doctor who made the diagnosis, and who understands the problem, performing the surgery.

☐ Insist on a business level deliverable that communicates your risk in business language. It should have clear steps of action based on real findings. Not general, one-size-fits-all recommendations.

Keep Your Team Up-To-Date on Relevant Threats, Not Just Laws

☐ If you are using an outside firm to manage your security, require quarterly updates on what hackers are doing to gain access. New tactics are being created daily, and are used for a period of time until people start to catch on. Then they change. You need to know what's going on.

☐ Read! The CIO section of *The Wall Street Journal, (Online Version)*, provides a business level explanation of the tactics being used by scammers. *Dark Reading (Online Resource)* and *Krebs on Security, (Blog)*, will provide more details for those who want them.

Look to Detection, Not to Your Checklist

- ☐ When your compliance checklist is complete, congratulate yourself on a job well done. But don't stop your security planning.

- ☐ Make sure your business is set up with security breach detection technologies. UTM firewalls, SIEM technology, and ongoing monitoring from a security operations center are all things to consider.

- ☐ Monitor insider activity, both visually and through automation. Train your team to spot violations internally, and give them clear direction and incentive to report it.

ACTION ITEMS TO MOVE TOWARD REAL SECURITY

- ✓ Give compliance serious attention. Get it done.
- ✓ Create a separate initiative to secure your data.
- ✓ Contract with professional security experts to assess your risk, measuring impact vs. likelihood.
- ✓ Take action on the reports they deliver, cleaning up any symptoms of a breach, and shoring up any vulnerabilities noted in their report.
- ✓ Create a continuous user awareness program to keep your team up to date on what hackers and scammers are doing to steal and misuse data.

Getting Your Company Focused on Security vs. Compliance

Remember, money is digital, and data is worth money. Your team must understand the value of the data they create and use, where compliance fits in, and how scammers and hackers are going to get around compliance-required controls to access your data. This is where the breach will happen.

Complete Any Outstanding Compliance Tasks

☐ Have a team charged with maintaining compliance. Even if it's the same team, treat it as a separate project.

☐ Document your program and educate your team on what compliance is.

Complete a Full Risk Assessment

☐ Use quarterly security assessments to evaluate the true exposure of your company.

☐ Insist on business-level findings and reporting.

☐ Create an initiative to secure all reported vulnerabilities according to priority.

Provide Ongoing User Awareness

☐ Provide education on both compliance and security to your team.

☐ Encourage your team to handle data securely, understanding that compliance grows every time a business is breached. This ends up costing businesses like yours more money, without necessarily making your data any more secure.

☐ Maintain and require the reading and sign-off of all security policies.

CHAPTER FOURTEEN

Mindset Three: Security is an Enabler

Sometimes it feels like data security is your greatest business inhibitor. Done right, security is the thing that enables the rock climber to scale large walls, and race car drivers to travel at breakneck speeds without dying.

On weekends, while attending college in Philadelphia, I would often drive up to Ralph Stover Park, The Red Rocks of the East Coast, rock to climb.

Being in college, I was on a tight budget. But instead of eating out and buying trendy clothing, I poured what little funds I had into climbing ropes, carabiners, harnesses, and chocks, (used for lead climbing). Flipping through the REI, (Recreational Equipment Inc.), catalogue was thrilling. I would sit there dreaming about my next purchase, while saving my pennies.

If you've never climbed a rock wall, it's amazing. I've watched people free climb, (no ropes). It too is amazing to watch, but you'll never catch me out there. One fall, and it's all over. And I've taken my share of falls, but always with the right safety gear to save me.

In most cases, unless doing an aided climb, you don't actually use the ropes or the hardware. They're there to catch you if you fall. Without them, you would die. For me, they weren't cumbersome. They brought comfort. They were the thing that allowed me to go from a dull walk in the park, to hanging backwards off of a death-defying cliff. Red Rocks isn't all that high, maybe 110 feet high at its highest point, but one fall will kill you. Without the safety equipment, I wouldn't recommend it.

Racing is similar. My home is right outside of Charlotte, NC, the NASCAR capital of the world. Drivers negotiate this track at breakneck speeds exceeding 180 mph. They wear helmets, harnesses, and fire-resistant suits, in case of a wreck. I believe they look forward to suiting up for the race, as the adrenaline in their bodies prepares them to do something most of us would not do. You wouldn't drive these speeds in a regular car on your local highway.

In both cases, the safety equipment is an enabler.

The Traditional Mindset: Security is an Expensive Business Inhibitor

The traditional mindset is, "We've got it covered." I hear this all the time. More security is expensive and unnecessary. The average business leader doesn't see anything that would indicate a problem, so the assumption is that everything is okay. Here are some signs that your organization has the wrong mindset.

☐ Your IT people are always saying, "We've got it covered," when asked about security breaches and trends.

☐ End-users roll their eyes when it's time to change passwords again.

☐ People are frustrated when they have to work through a VPN connection (Virtual Private Network. Encryption.)

- ☐ You hear complaints about not being able to send data through email. You discover people are doing it anyway because they don't have time to follow the rules.

- ☐ People refuse to come up with separate passwords for their various systems and online accounts.

- ☐ The passwords are simple: pet names, a spouse's name, etc.

- ☐ Security purchases are last in line because there is no measureable ROI, (Return on Investment).

The Enablement Mindset Defined: Security Allows Me to do Crazy Things That Put Our Company Ahead of the Competition

Perhaps you haven't thought about it quite like this, but security is an enabler. Think of it as safety. It's not insurance.

Both the climber and the driver are likely insured. In a major accident, they pull out their policy to help offset healthcare costs. If things really go south, their life insurance policy kicks in to help their family stay afloat, (disability, or worst case, life insurance).

Hopefully your insurance pays if a major problem occurs.

But safety equipment is not insurance. It is used to prevent a tragedy from ever happening in the first place.

Your company can purchase cyber-insurance in case your safety net fails. But my goal is to help you put the right security in place, so that you'll never need to file that claim.

Using the right security controls, you and your team can do incredible things that can put your company ahead of your competition, expand your global reach, bring you closer to your customers, and speed up time to market, while giving you the agile work environment you need to thrive in today's fast-changing market.

☐ Suddenly, you can access your bank, deposit checks, transfer money, and manage your investments, all on your phone, while on the run, or standing in a busy airport. Just be careful about who is standing behind you, and don't use the free Wi-Fi system (use your cell phone hot spot which is much safer).

☐ You can work out of a hotel in a room right next to your competition while attending a tradeshow, creating and accessing quotes, sending invoices, and exchanging ideas. But make sure you understand how to protect these documents when operating on a "very" public network. Note: If you happen to be attending a security / white hat hackers conference, don't use the public networks.

☐ You can shop using credit cards and other electronic payment systems without the fear of your bank account being taken over.

☐ You can work almost anywhere. In your car, hotel, coffee shop, airport, etc. No longer do you need to be sitting in the office behind a firewall to access sensitive data.

☐ You can leverage inexpensive virtual assistants, who work remotely and are likely more cost effective than hiring someone locally.

☐ Instead of complaining about passwords that have to be updated, you understand how cool it is that you can do all of the above things. Suddenly, changing a password is a small price to pay for this kind of convenience. And now, with your new password vault, it's not really that cumbersome.

Note: As I've stated earlier in the book, if you're connected, your data is vulnerable. However, with the right security controls in place, working at the airport can be almost as safe as working in your office. Both can be compromised, but the likelihood is greatly reduced when properly secured. Especially if you take my advice and use your cell phone hot spot.

Adopting the Right Mindset: Security is an Enabler

This mindset may take some cultivating, but if you take the time to show people what the risks are, and then show them the controls that prevent disaster, you can move the entire organization closer to the enabler mindset. IT can't be the sole protector of data. It requires everyone's buy-in.

Security Enables, but Computing in Public Without Proper Security is Foolish

☐ Don't be fooled. Computing in public places without the proper security controls is unwise.

☐ Beware of fake hotspots. These are rogue access points, set up to lure you to someone's personal network, with the intent to take your data. It's easy to do, and people do it every day.

☐ Just because a public network exists doesn't mean you should connect to it.

☐ Hotel networks are handy, but easily compromised - especially at an event designed for hundreds or thousands of competitors.

☐ If you ever attend a conference for security professionals, don't bother using that public network. It's not safe.

Use Password Vaults for Better Security

We've covered this topic already. If you're going mobile, you need better passwords. Use your newly installed password vault software to enhance your security posture. Every user should have one.

Protect Document Transmission with Tools Like Capsule and Secure Email

☐ Capsule, a software tool put out by Check Point Software, is one example of a secure transmission application. Most email is clear-text, meaning anyone can read the transmission. Capsule-like products wrap the data you want to send in a secure package. The person on the receiving end will need a password (or key) to open it. Unauthorized users will have a hard time getting past this extra layer of protection (although it is still possible).

☐ Move away from POP3 and other free email tools. POP3 is a way of downloading email. It's not secure. Free email tools such as Juno, Hotmail, etc., are more likely to be compromised. All businesses should be on a private, hosted email domain with adequate content filtering and spam controls.

☐ For greater security, use email products designed for secure transmission using encryption. Secure documents should be transmitted using tools like Capsule, or through a secure email system such as *Protected Trust, (protectedtrust.com)*.

Secure Your Phone or Tablet, And Go Mobile

☐ Lock your phone. It should be password protected and set to delete itself after a number of tries. Make sure you have a backup. Remember it can be broken into, so don't lose it.

☐ Use mobile security software. Mobile Device Management software was designed to centrally manage phones in a corporate environment. Don't confuse this with security. Mobile security software detects malware that might creep in through the app store, a scan code, or infected websites and spam email.

☐ Enable your software firewall; something we've already discussed.

Use the Cloud, (Wisely)

☐ Use the cloud, taking note of my earlier comments on using respectable cloud providers. If your data is in the cloud, you have a real-time copy. If your phone is lost or stolen, you will still have your data. But remember, someone else may also have that data through your compromised phone.

Make Use of Your Personal Hotspot

☐ For those times where a reputable Wi-Fi network is not available, consider using your phone's hotspot feature. Hotspot uses your cellphone carrier network and is encrypted. While nothing is completely secure, your personal hotspot is far more secure than a hotel or coffee shop network. Although it will cost you if you run out of data on any given month, the tradeoff is worth it. If you avoid watching videos on this connection, you should be okay.

Getting Your Company Focused on Security Enablement

When your team understands the value of data, and how scammers use it to make money, they will be more likely to comply with company security policies. Ignore this, and your team members will be irritated by all of the rules, passwords, and bureaucracy. Education is the first step to building the right mindset.

Show Your Team What the Hackers Are Up To

☐ Make it personal. When your office workers see what scammers are doing to steal from individuals, they start to realize that it applies to them. Awareness is the first step. Stories will bring it to life.

☐ Keep them up to date on scams through news bulletins, stories, and regular training videos.

Equip Your Team, Creating Greater Efficiency

- ☐ Set up policies that govern the creation and usage of data outside of the office. You can't leave this up to your end-users.

- ☐ Centrally managed software should be deployed on mobile devices to stop malware and misuse.

- ☐ Segmenting personal devices protects the end-user's personal data such as music, family photos, social media, and personal applications.

Go Mobile

- ☐ Encourage your team to be mobile. Equip them with lightweight, easy to use tablets and laptops. With the right equipment, your team will be more likely to stay connected when not in the office.

CHAPTER FIFTEEN

Mindset Four: Secrets Should be Kept Secret

Everything you do in life leaves a trail of data. Some of that data is extremely personal. You have financial data, customer data, product data, and more. Both your business and your personal life can be described by the data trail you leave. Make sure you know where it is, what it is, and who has access to it.

How much do the people around you know about you? What about your spouse, your kids, your co-workers, your pastor…or your competition? It turns out that with all of these technology advancements, it's getting harder to keep secrets. Privacy is dying out.

Earlier, I mentioned Edward Snowden. According to Snowden, the NSA uses technology to search online databases, emails, chat boards, and your browsing history, all without authorization. The tool is called XKeyscore. Google it, and you'll be surprised at what you discover.

Remember what Snowden told us, (repeating from earlier in the book), "I, sitting at my desk, can wiretap anyone, from you or your accountant, to a federal judge or even the president, if I have a personal email."

Since Snowden, a huge amount of attention has been paid to government snooping. However, it's not just the government who's collecting data. There's a much greater and more immediate threat to your privacy, and it's coming from companies you've probably never heard of. They're called data brokers.

Data brokers collect and analyze your most sensitive, personal information, and then sell it online. They sell it to each other, to advertisers, to social media sites, and even to the government.

This has been going on for years. Every purchase you make, all of the data collected through online forms, rewards cards, sweepstakes entries, and even web searches…it's all recorded and compiled. This is called *data aggregation*, and it's a powerful thing.

They have your name, address, special dates, purchasing habits, and browsing habits, and they know how you respond to advertising. From this data, they know your likes, dislikes, lifestyle habits, and even your daily movements. They can even predict things about you and how you think, and surmise things about you that your closest family members have no knowledge of.

Acxiom is currently the largest data broker in the world. They claim to know just about everything about you, having on record about 1,500 data items on any given individual in the U.S.

What kinds of information are either taken or derived? Your religion, ethnicity, political affiliations, user names, income, and family medical history, (e.g. addictions, depression and other psychological conditions, medications, etc.), sexual orientation, places you frequent, and more. From the data created when you do something, (just about anything), big data aggregation engines can derive all kinds of things about you. In some cases, these programs have guessed a woman was pregnant before she herself even knew about it! This is scary stuff.

As an example, *Statlistic,* a company headquartered in the northeast, advertises lists of gay and lesbian adults and people suffering from bipolar disorders. These people may or may not have disclosed their alternate lifestyle, yet the computer knows, and is willing to sell that information to the right buyer.

Another one, *Paramount Lists*, sells the names of people with alcohol, sexual, and gambling addictions, as well as the names of people desperate to get out of debt. *Exact Data*, advertises lists of people who have a sexually transmitted disease, or who purchase pornography and sex toys. This data comes from stores and sites you browse or shop on. Your data is collected and sold as another revenue stream, and you can assume that all of the stores you use do this. That data, aggregated and analyzed against all of the other data you generate, allows *deep machine learning computers* to predict, guess, and profile all kinds of things you had no intention of revealing. And it's more accurate than you might think.

The Traditional Mindset: Passwords Work, My Accounts are Private, and Data Exposure isn't a Big Deal

☐ People are posting all kinds of daily events, their upcoming vacation plans, and more, on social media. This alone opens a large door into your world. The assumption is, this is public information which, if seen, is harmless.

☐ Email is considered a private messaging service, as well as texting and Facebooking. The assumption is, no one would ever read my email.

☐ End-users are surprised when someone finds out they've been accessing pornography or other restricted materials on company time.

☐ Managers complain that they can no longer access "Certain Unnamed sites" after a recent security upgrade.

☐ People continue sending credit card numbers with expiration dates and security code numbers through email.

☐ The people around you believe that their medical history is safe in the EMR system.

☐ People email tax files to their accountant, along with other financial or insurance related documents.

The Secret Mindset Defined: Today's Digitalized World Requires Extra Steps to Keep Secrets Secret

The things I've just listed should be a wakeup call. It might even stir up some anger. Your privacy has been invaded in ways you can't imagine. According to the Wall Street Journal, those of the younger generation assume their data is out there and minimize the potential impact.

If people are willing to reveal their entire lives online without concern, what are they doing with corporate data? The data that must remain a secret in order to effectively compete? Or data that threatens to bring major lawsuits against your company if revealed?

The Secret Mindset is a "Need-to-Know" mindset. It says that if someone doesn't need this data, they don't have access to it. If it doesn't need to be online, don't put it online. In many cases, the higher up the organization chart one goes, the greater access a person will demand. This is a wrong mindset. What does this mindset really mean to you and your organization?

- ☐ With this mindset, you understand that one piece of data may be meaningless, but aggregated data is powerful, and can lead to all kinds of insights, predictions, and revelations you don't want to disclose.

- ☐ You also know that your data is not an island. It's all being aggregated in one place. Your life is being pieced together and used by others, possibly to manipulate you, your buying habits, and even your political and religious belief systems.

- ☐ Secrecy carries over to your business. Your competition, other governments, and anyone who stands to make money stealing and reselling your intellectual property, can access it. The more data you put out there, the more vulnerable you are.

- ☐ You should only give access when someone needs access to get their job done. Sometimes that access can be temporary. When that's the case, only give temporary access.

- ☐ Levels of access are defined according to security policies. So one person might have read-only access, while another might have the ability to edit certain data, but not delete it. Others might have access to part of the data, but not all of it. And still others might have full access to read, edit, add, and delete your data.

☐ At some level, data access should be monitored. With this mindset, the organization understands that accountability should be required. Monitor the usage of those authorized to access data. No one is beyond temptation when circumstances are bad. The organization must accept some level of oversite to keep everyone honest.

☐ Some information should NOT be put in digital format on connected systems. This is especially true for some government related systems. If it's connected, it is accessible.

Adopting the Right Mindset: Secrets Need to be Kept Secret

Classify Your Data

☐ We've discussed this already, but all data should be classified, dictating how it is handled, stored, transmitted, and who can access it.

Create Separations of Duty

Nuclear launch codes provide us with a clear example of separation of duty. No one person can launch a weapon of this magnitude in the US. Hopefully that is the case anywhere a weapon of mass destruction exists.

☐ More than one person should be required to make major system changes or access highly sensitive data. This is especially true where IT workers have access to maintain systems of a highly sensitive nature.

☐ Financial systems should always require multiple people to transfer large sums of money.

Restrict Access & Maintain Access Control Over an Employee's Lifecycle

☐ Access to data is given according to one's job responsibility.

☐ Access should be limited to what that person needs on a regular basis. If the employee requires READ access, they should not have the ability to EDIT.

☐ Require higher levels of authorization when a higher access privilege is needed. For instance, a cashier may require the manager to enter a password before a large return can be made.

☐ When roles and positions change, access must also change. It should be part of the transition procedure to review access and make sure that an employee in a new role, has only the access they need for that role.

☐ Exiting employees should be cut off from access immediately upon resignation or termination. I recommend, when possible, not having an exiting employee fulfill a two week notice. Rather, cut off access immediately. I suspect that it is during these two weeks that most internal theft takes place.

Monitor Access and Usage

☐ Most computers today allow for some type of journaling. Use it.

☐ Systems used for highly sensitive transactions should be monitored using software that logs activities and keystrokes, and records snap shots under certain circumstances. This is not expensive to do, but may provide the accountability you need to keep people from stealing money and intellectual capital.

☐ Closely monitor all third-party access such as contractors working with sensitive data. During development and early testing on applications, test data should be used in place of production data.

Educate Users on Their Data Trail & How to Respond to Requests

☐ All of us are leaving a data trail with our phones, GPS, purchases, etc. Users should be educated on what activities are creating data, and how to reduce the amount of data being created.

☐ Scammers will use social engineering skills to talk busy office workers into giving access. There should be a clear, simple, escalation procedure in place to prevent the disclosure of sensitive data. Note: *The Art of Deception,* By Kevin Mitnik provides some helpful insights on how easy it is for scammers to convince someone to bypass their escalation procedures.

ACTION ITEMS TO ENABLE YOUR BUSINESS WITH SECURITY

✓ Make sure your data is clearly classified with procedures and guidelines that govern usage, access, transmission, access privileges, as well as storage, archival, and deletion requirements.

✓ Separate duties for access and handling of sensitive data.

✓ Restrict activities regarding highly sensitive data to specified systems that can be monitored for unauthorized access or activities.

✓ Deploy centralized access control tools to restrict and manage access through the lifecycle of each employee.

✓ Provide ongoing security awareness training on how end-users can minimize data trails, and how to respond to requests that may lead to data misuse or theft.

Getting Your Company Focused on Security Enablement

Educate Your Team on Data Leakage Issues

☐ Data leakage usually occurs when well-meaning employees get too busy. They may be responding to customer needs, trying to fulfill requests for management more quickly, or looking for an easy way to continue working from home to meet deadlines.

Show Your Team How Data Aggregators Are Using Data

☐ The more your team understands about how their own lives are being compromised digitally, the more aware they will be as they handle sensitive, company data.

☐ Educate them on how computers are able to derive information from aggregated data. Few people understand the power computers have when it comes to predicting something. Big Data systems have been praised for their ability to interview candidates far more effectively than an actual human, face-to-face interview. With aggregated data, they can figure out more about a person in a fraction of a second, than a real person with years of interviewing experience.

☐ Make sure your employees understand what your competition wants to know. Few workers really understand their company's strategy, and what keeps them ahead of the competition.

Explain Why it is to Their Benefit to Have Greater Control and Accountability

☐ People don't like accountability. However, when theft occurs, it is helpful to have enough data to prove your innocence. Help your employees see why this is critical in the case of computers and sensitive data.

☐ Develop a culture of accountability. Your team should know how to identify misuse, be willing to do something about it, and know what to do about it.

Equip Your Company With the Tools Needed to Guard Against Data Leaks and the Theft of Intellectual Capital

☐ Begin building detection and monitoring into your networks and computers.

☐ Use data leakage software, configured with policies that detect certain types of data, before they leave your network through clear-text email or other data transfer programs.

☐ Prevent the storage of highly sensitive data on mobile devices through data leakage policies.

CHAPTER SIXTEEN

Mindset Five: The Bad Guys Can Always Get In

If it's connected, it can be accessed. Firewalls, passwords, and encryption are all good things, but don't be fooled. All data is accessible if someone really wants it. The question should never be, "Can we keep them out?" Instead, create tripwires for early detection.

A few years ago I read a story of a man in a small town out west entering an engineering firm. When he arrived, he asked for the president of the company. He had flown in that morning for a lunch meeting to discuss a joint venture opportunity.

When he asked for Jim, the president, the front desk attendee apologetically informed him that Jim was on vacation until the end of the week. The weary traveler was stunned. He had just flown across the US for this meeting. There must be some mistake.

Pulling out his calendar, he showed the attendee his appointment entry. But the attendant again apologized. There was nothing she could do. The traveler then sifted through his email, finding the exchange that had occurred while setting up the appointment, and realized it was supposed to be next week. Now what?

In a last ditch effort he asked if he could take some of the engineers out to lunch to exchange some ideas, and then reschedule his appointment with the president. It sounded like a good plan, and the attendant was happy to gather the group.

With detailed designs in hand, they headed out to lunch to talk shop. The traveler shared with them how Jim and he were planning to partner on this development effort. They reviewed the details, and at the end of the lunch, the traveler asked for copies of the plans. The engineers gladly handed them over. They'd catch up next week and he would return them when he came to meet with Jim.

Monday morning, Jim was in the office early in hopes of catching up on some email. His lead engineer stopped by to share his excitement about the joint venture. Jim had no idea what he was talking about. They would never get their design documents back. It was a scam.

How do you defend against stuff like this? Your team must begin building the mindset that says, "They can always get in."

The Traditional Mindset: We're Behind the Firewall

The average business person believes that being behind a firewall means their data is safe. They also believe that they would know it if their data were under attack or being accessed by unauthorized people. Here are some of the signs that your company is operating with the wrong mindset.

☐ You think your network is safe because you have a firewall.

☐ When asked about security, you reply, "We've got it covered," simply because you have not seen any malicious activity.

☐ You believe a successful pen-test means your company can't be hacked into.

☐ You open emails from people you don't know and click on attachments without knowing who they came from.

☐ You indiscriminately surf the web, clicking on links that sound good without ever thinking, "This could be a trap."

☐ You respond to emails without thinking, "This might be a scam."

☐ You download apps and send confidential information via email, without a second thought.

☐ You believe IT has it covered, and therefore, you can do your job without thinking about security.

The "They Can Get In" Mindset Defined: People Can Always Get In

You've been told by security companies that their technology will keep you safe. It's true that security products can greatly reduce the likelihood of intrusion. But there are no technologies that can guarantee security. This mindset understands:

☐ Firewalls block ports, but they also have holes for email, web traffic, and more. Hackers can disguise their traffic to look like legitimate traffic.

☐ Email can always get in. You understand that many hacks involve sending malware in through an email attachment or embedded link.

☐ Malware does not have to be clicked on to execute.

☐ Big corporate websites, like your online banking site, can be compromised.

☐ Pen tests are used to see if hackers can gain access. They fall short when they don't consider the primary ways hackers get in, mainly social engineering.

☐ Social engineers can always find a way in. It's human nature to believe people when they say they are authorized, or work in another department.

☐ The person with this mindset expects people to be coming in. Rather than thinking everything is safe, they are constantly on the alert.

Adopting the Right Mindset: People Can Get in, it's Our Job to Detect Them Before it's too Late

Who's job is it to keep your data safe? It's Everyone's job. Your organization cannot assume IT has it covered. Instead, each user must be on the lookout, just like they would be when walking through a large city. The police can't protect every citizen, every moment of the day. They're just part of the response plan, and generally, late to the party. Note: this is not a slam on law enforcement. I'm merely pointing out that people misunderstand their role in society.

Firewalls Don't Work

Continuing to operate with the misconception that *firewalls and passwords keep people out* will lead to more data theft. The first step is agreeing that there's always a way to get in.

☐ Firewalls are filters full of holes. They screen out the obvious bad stuff, but not intelligent malware. Note: More advanced firewalls, including Check Point, Palo Alto, Cisco's ASA, Fortinet, and some other mainstream appliances offer add-ons through software to detect these threats, but few IT people really understand them.

☐ Passwords are easily hacked using dictionary attacks, key loggers, and compromised passwords from hacked sites.

☐ Easy passwords can be guessed using sophisticated algorithms that analyze social media sites to figure out what a user might choose.

☐ A recent study showed that spoken commands can take over a smartphone set up with tools like, *"Hey Siri."*

☐ Encryption can be bypassed at the end-node or decrypted. Given enough time hackers will get in.

Use Continuous Assessments

☐ Risk assessments should be ongoing. PCI requires some companies to scan once each year. Higher transaction companies scan four times per year. Neither is adequate.

☐ Assessing means more than scanning networks. Company leadership should know where their data is, what is important, what their top three to five threats are, and how they are trending. They need the Impact vs. Likelihood graph.

Be Alert When Accessing Public Wi-Fi

☐ When using public Wi-Fi, care should be given to what networks you are actually connected to, and if that network is in fact controlled by the store or shop you are in.

☐ Avoid accessing highly sensitive data over public networks. If you must access your bank now, use your personal hotspot. Assume the people around you are watching you.

☐ Public networks should not be used without adequate system level security. The larger the network, the less likely you are to know if someone out there is working to compromise your data.

Be on Guard When Accessing Websites and Reading Email

☐ Websites, even those from reputable companies such as banks and investment firms, are vulnerable. When these sites are compromised, it is generally detected quickly. However, accessing that site before they remediate could result in a compromise. You won't know it until it's too late. If something doesn't look right, contact the company before continuing.

☐ When receiving email from banks and financial companies with links to click on, don't click. Instead, contact customer service to follow up on anything they need from you.

☐ Don't click on unexpected attachments or emails from people you don't know.

☐ Use aggressive spam filters to clean out obvious scams and unwanted email.

☐ Use corporate email systems. If you use something that's free for personal email, use mainline email services such as Gmail. Avoid using POP3 email protocols.

Enable Personal Device Security Tools

☐ Enable personal software firewalls.

☐ Keep software and antivirus programs up to date.

☐ Protect mobile devices, including phones and tablets, with security software.

✓ Schedule your next security / risk assessment now.
✓ Educate users on Wi-Fi usage and how compromise happens.
✓ Educate users on email and website compromise, and best practices to avoid them.
✓ Make sure your company is guarding against web threats. Deploy content filtering software to reduce the likelihood of infected websites compromising your company systems.
✓ Deploy mobile security to all end-node devices such as phones and tablets.

Getting Your Company Focused on Security Enablement

Improve Your P-Column Security

☐ Upgrade your passwords using at least 8 characters, alpha-numeric combinations, and special characters. Use password vaults and password generators for better security.

☐ Make sure firewalls are up-to-date, with the proper rules and restrictions configured.

☐ Use encryption. Disks, backups, phones, and tablets should all be encrypted.

☐ Use VPN technology and encrypt all sensitive communication.

Destroy Old Data

☐ With inexpensive storage, the tendency is to save all data. Don't do it! Instead, specify data archival and retention policies, deleting old data that is no longer required. Note: Data that is deleted just before a lawsuit will lead to suspicion. If your deletion policies are followed, you can't be held liable unless the data you've deleted has a legal restriction for archiving.

☐ When upgrading, old systems should be destroyed, including hard drives.

☐ Personal devices should be wiped when employees leave. In most cases this will require special software to segment these devices. Remember, deleted data is not really deleted. It's just hidden until it is overwritten.

CHAPTER SEVENTEEN

Mindset Six: Assume People Are In

Detection is the most important aspect of data security and it starts with you. If you don't expect people to be watching, you'll stop looking. In a connected world, there are people who want your data every day. Get in the habit of looking, interrogating, and requiring people to show their credentials.

The people around you are watching. If your security people are telling you everything is great, don't believe them. Instead, tell them to keep looking. Good security involves great detection.

The Traditional Mindset: No One Cares

Whether you think people can't see your data, or you think no one cares, both are wrong mindsets. Signs that your company is operating with a wrong belief system include:

☐ "No one cares about our small company. We just make
_____ ,(Fill in your company's widgets,) parts."

☐ "My Facebook page isn't that interesting. No one is reading
this stuff except my friends."

☐ "There's so much data online, who would possibly take the
time to look at my data?"

☐ "The people in our company are trustworthy. They won't be
poking around, looking at payroll or other sensitive data."

☐ "The IT guys won't do anything they're not supposed to do.
Neither will my friends, people I've worked with for years,
or my employees."

The "People are Watching" Mindset Defined: Automation and Aggregation Make All Data a Target

Your data is worth money. Remember, *digital money* doesn't just mean currency. Your data is money. Often, data that may not be worth much to you, such as your healthcare information, is worth a fortune to someone else.

I've also discussed *data aggregation*. One data element, by itself, may be useless. But put thousands of data elements together, and out pops something you've never considered.

Go on eBay. You'll find just about anything for sale. This site should be illegal. It's a pawn shop without accountability. If you steal from your neighbor and take their stereo or diamond necklace to the pawnshop, that dealer has to register your items. If your neighbor has registered serial numbers and pictures on their local law enforcement portal, that merchandise leads right back to you. Expect to be arrested.

On eBay, this doesn't happen. There are no registrations, and since the buyer could be anywhere in the world, the chances of getting caught are slim.

Search for some expensive medical equipment. Chances are you can find a deal on one of those multi-thousand dollar scooters. Where did it come from? It's listed as new or like-new. Chances are, the person selling that thing bought it using fraudulent medical data, paid for by someone's healthcare insurance.

How about that new MacPro laptop? In many cases that "new" laptop doesn't actually exist yet. You bid, make the purchase, and the seller will take a compromised credit card, buy the computer, and send it to you. They can afford to sell it at a steep discount since they are getting it for free. The banks are quick these days. They'll cancel that credit card immediately. But the seller just made $2000 on that one purchase. It's likely that they paid between $5 and $10 to get that card, depending on how good the card is. It's a high margin business for the hacker, and it's tax free money.

In today's crime market, hackers are willing to take any data they can get their hands on. Capturing data can be automated, so the idea is to grab whatever you can find, and sort it out later. From there, hackers come up with scams to make money using whatever data they have.

☐ The Wall Street Journal reports, "Every major network in the country has been compromised." Do you believe it?

☐ Most of the small networks I see being assessed have botware on them. This means that unauthorized users have installed software that gives them access to that system. If one computer in your company is infected, the bot owner has access.

☐ The FBI tells us that the average company finds out 14 months too late that they have been compromised. Chances are, you won't know until it's too late.

☐ Don't be surprised if you find malware or signs of unauthorized access. Be surprised if everything looks clean. Then consider having someone else take a look.

☐ If the hackers aren't watching, marketers are. Marketing intelligence is growing faster than just about anything I know of. Shop for something, don't buy it, and you'll start to see ads popping up on your Facebook and LinkedIn pages. It's all connected. This type of data isn't illegal. However, the profile they are building should be cause for caution.

Adopting the Right Mindset: People Are Looking at My Data

Even if they are not in your computer right now, people are looking at your aggregated data, at least from a big data perspective. But it gets worse. They are also likely trying to get access to your personal computer.

The right mindset assumes that there are automated hacking tools out there, searching the Internet for systems that can be easily compromised. Assessing your risk with the right mindset is essential to getting an accurate picture of risk.

Assessments Reveal Impact and Likelihood, Not Untouchable Data

☐ Assessments almost always reveal problems. Make sure your assessors are checking for malicious traffic. Most don't. If you have computers reaching out to servers in Russia, that might be an indication.

☐ Pen-testing should be used to pin point a vulnerability. It is not a test for whether something can be accessed. Your data can always be accessed with enough social engineering effort.

☐ Assessments should identify data value, where data is, who has access, and what relevant threats exist. The final deliverable should provide a measure of likelihood. What are the odds that this data will be compromised?

☐ Security threats constantly change. Assume hackers are always one step ahead. The assessment should target symptoms of a breach, and then provide instructions on how to close that hole in the armor.

☐ The assessment should also determine how likely it is that your team will be able to detect a breach, and respond before it is too late.

Early Detection Requires Specialized Tools

Great security assumes the door will be breached. Detection must be nearly perfect, and highly automated.

☐ Don't assume people are looking at logs and reports. Computers generate millions of journal entries every day. A human being cannot analyze this data manually. If your IT people tell you they are watching the logs, it might be worth a trip to the computer center to see exactly what that means.

☐ Detection tools must be able to look inside the data that is encrypted. They must also be able to execute macros and other executables that are attached to email. This is done using a "sandbox" technology built to execute and detect anything malicious.

☐ All incoming connections should be analyzed before a session is granted to any user. Technologies such as NAC (Network Access Control), give companies the ability to check out computers that are requesting access. Any system with outdated AV or other software can be forced to upgrade prior to granting a session.

☐ Computers are good at log analysis. However, someone with security experience must be able to piece together alerts to determine if the company is under attack, or a false positive exists. In most cases, I recommend using a third party to do this. Highly trained security professionals are hard to come by in midsized and small businesses.

Note: Even if a small business could attract and pay for top security talent, the lack of actual security events would put that person in a holding pattern for a year, to the point where their skills were no longer up to date.

Data Aggregation is Used by Hackers; You Can Also Use It

In 2015, the Office of Personnel Management, (OPM), was hacked. Donna Seymour, OPM's then current CISO, was questioned as to why this happened. Her response? "Our equipment was outdated."

More questions should have been asked. Why was it outdated? Probably because they didn't have a sufficient budget. But why? Probably because Donna didn't have a clearly written Impact vs. Likelihood Graph. Without an understanding of likelihood, she had little justification to spend the money. But the cleanup is always far more expensive.

The fallout is far more important. The initial reports suggested that this data was not all that significant. But after further investigation, people started to realize the power of data aggregation. Other hacks, which may have been initiated by the same group against airlines and other travel data followed. What was going on? Perhaps hackers from nation-states or terrorist cells were using this data to figure out who the US undercover agents were, and where they might be.

As this story unfolded, it became clear that families all over the world, related to agents and other key roles, were suddenly at risk. Data revealing FBI, CIA, NSA, and DoD personnel, was now exposed.

It's unknown at this point what the real impact of this breach was, but the future of data science and big data analytics makes this type of hack a major threat to both personal and national security.

☐ Data value changes through aggregation. Take steps to reduce the amount of data accessible to people outside the company.

☐ Data aggregation can also be used internally to predict or provide early detection of an intrusion. Technology such as SEIM systems are often the best way to detect malware or web-threats coming in through email, infected websites, or compromised VPN sessions.

☐ Your end-users should be educated on the value of data and the reality of data aggregation, and equipped with an understanding of who would want this data, and what a breach would mean to the company.

Prepare Users to Respond

☐ Finally, being able to respond means equipping your team to respond in real time.

☐ Users should know what represents misuse and unauthorized access. They need to understand why it matters, be willing to report it, and know how to report it.

☐ If you're not seeing anything, look deeper. Keep looking until you find something. Expect it to be there.

ACTION ITEMS TO ENABLE YOUR BUSINESS WITH SECURITY
✓ Review your last assessment. Does it give you detailed analysis on how much risk you have? Did the team analyze data to discover symptoms of compromise?
✓ Implement a detection strategy. Begin adding technologies that detect and stop web-threats, malware, ransomware, and other botware.

✓ Educate your team on the value of data, the likelihood of automated systems and social engineering compromising their data, and the power of aggregated data to reveal things they've never considered.

✓ Make sure everyone knows how to detect a breach or unauthorized activity, and is willing to take action. Finally, make sure they know how to report it.

Getting Your Company Focused on Security Enablement. If People Are Looking, Something Must be Done

☐ Make sure your leadership team is involved in the assessment process. A thorough assessment takes into account the value of data, the competition, nation-states, and the current business environment. Consider M&A activities, lawsuits, new product announcements, layoffs and anything that might change the value of your company's data.

☐ Develop a culture of alertness. The more alert your team is to fraudulent phone calls and emails, the better.

☐ Help your team understand the value of data and aggregated data. This includes who would want your data, why it's important, and why its confidentiality, integrity, and availability matter to the company.

CHAPTER EIGHTEEN

Mindset Seven: Poised to Respond

> Detection is only as good as your response plan. Again, this starts with you. Your IT department can only take action if they know something's wrong. Many times, your early detection and willingness to respond will be the things that set security in motion. Don't be afraid to act.

On June 12, 2016 at 2 AM, the deadliest mass shooting in history took place at the Pulse Club in Orlando Florida. Federal authorities had investigated Omar Mateen long before this heinous killing spree, but without proper evidence, they discontinued their surveillance.

In the weeks that followed, conservative and liberal politicians fired back and forth on issues surrounding Internet surveillance, gun control, and second Amendment rights, freedom of speech and first amendment rights, and more.

In the attack, armed with a rifle and a handgun, Mateen managed to kill 49 people and injure over 50 before being taken down by SWAT teams.

Why did this happen? How can it be prevented in the future? And what does this have to do with data security?

Analysis: Security is Failing...Why?

The average mass shooting happens very quickly. As cited earlier, eleven minutes is the average, elapsed time of an active shooter attack. It's fast! That's not a long time to detect and respond, is it?

How long did Mateen's shooting spree last? The news reports weren't clear, but it was well before law enforcement could intervene. A local police department may take as long as twenty minutes to arrive once dispatched. If you do the math, you can see the disconnect. Law enforcement cannot stop an attack unless they know well beforehand that it will happen. Unfortunately, in most cases, they don't.

Remember, the police force does not exist to protect you as an individual. They're not body guards. And the current counterterrorist techniques which fall into the jurisdiction of agencies like the FBI, are not that great at finding and stopping individuals like Mateen (a man not completely associated with ISIS, but acting as if he were).

Experts agree that it's impossible to have enough resources to keep individuals safe. The FBI doesn't have the bandwidth, and the police are not set up for these types of situations.

It's a wrong mindset; a misunderstanding of roles. And when security is approached with the wrong mindset, it fails miserably.

Could the Florida Mass Shooting Have Been Prevented?

Early reports on the Florida massacre suggested that Mateen was acting as an individual who had been converted through ISIS's online propaganda, (i.e. Facebook). ISIS did not plan the attack; Mateen did. However, he was apparently acting on what he believed ISIS would approve.

As soon as the attack was over, the political bashing began. It's a tragedy for sure, and when tragedy occurs, it's easy to point the finger and say that the current system is broken. But I believe this was simply a mistake made by the club itself. Let me explain.

One FBI Agent I spoke with referred to Club Pulse as a *Soft Target*. This simply means, Club Pulse was defenseless against this type of attack. That's probably because, up until about a year ago, these types of attacks were extremely rare. You'll remember earlier in the book, I suggested that, at large, our society lives by the belief that everyone is good. We're a trusting society. The assumption is that an attack like this is unlikely, and therefore no one is prepared for it. Club Pulse could have been prepared, but without a clear measure of risk, an impact vs. likelihood graph, or physical security, they were operating out of ignorance.

If they had done a study, they might have concluded that their risk was low. There's no need to staff on premise, armed guards. Had they determined their risk to be high, the expense would have been justified. You might be thinking that this type of risk analysis isn't possible; you're wrong. Most organizations will not take the time or spend the money to access risk. If terrorism continues to grow (and I believe it will), given our government's current policies and strategies, organizations like Club Pulse will need to conduct this type of risk analysis and be prepared to defend their clients in the future. You might be thinking, "We shouldn't have to do this," but the truth is, we've allowed this type of criminal behavior to emerge and grow in power. Wishing it would go away won't protect you from the next mass shooting.

Some questions are worth considering.

Is This the Fault of Law Enforcement?

News reports are not suggesting that this is the fault of the FBI or local law enforcement. However, the FBI certainly did all they could to cover their tracks. Recent news reports detailed some of their recent investigations of Mateen, revealing that they believed he might have had ties to terrorist organizations, namely ISIS. So they were involved early on.

Nothing ever came of the FBI's investigation. They didn't find anything conclusive. As an American Citizen, Mateen had rights, as he should. The FBI does not have the right to continue surveillance when a person is cleared of any wrong doing, (although, according to Snowden, that's no guarantee). None of us want to have the FBI, NSA, or any other government agency watching our every move if we're innocent. It's unclear, but either they assumed Mateen was completely harmless, or they didn't have the resources to continue watching him given other higher priority surveillance activities.

If the FBI followed their protocols as written (and we can only assume they did), they cannot be held responsible for this.

What about local law enforcement? The police are also not at fault. As we've already stated, (and it's been cited in many court cases), the police are not responsible to stop criminal acts. They can't be sitting in your front yard, or at Club Pulse, waiting for something to happen, unless there is probable cause to justify it. Law enforcement, in the words of our local police department, is responsible for, "Catching the bad guys." This is, of course, something that happens after a crime has been committed. If they get a lead or threat they'll do their best, but you can't expect them to cover fifty or a hundred threats or high-risk areas, in a single night.

Is Social Media the Problem?

What about social media? Mateen was apparently recruited over social media. At what point, we don't really know. His father, in an interview following the attack, had no knowledge of his radical beliefs. He stated, "This was not the result of religious beliefs."

Either he was in denial, or he just didn't know his son very well. Reports, and the 911 recording, confirm that Mateen was crying out to his god while carrying out the attack.

I'm not saying that all Muslims are on the attack. Rather, I'm pointing out that Mateen was someone who believed, in his warped perception of right and wrong, that he was doing this for Allah. He believed he was justified.

Apparently he made this ideological shift at some point with the encouragement of ISIS propaganda through Facebook and other social media sites. Is social media to blame? Of course not. Do we need more restrictions on what people can say online? If we do, your personal, religious views or political positions will be next. China does this. If people start questioning the government or subscribing to an unauthorized religion, the government stops them. Give away your freedom, and you'll never get it back, said Ben Franklin. Social media is not the root problem here.

Is the First Amendment at Fault?

Social media leads us right into a discussion on First Amendment Rights. Depending on what country you live in, you may or may not have the same rights.

Freedom of religion, speech, and the press are our rights as US citizens. However, if you're watching the news reports, there is a slow erosion taking place.

Can someone speak out against the US Government? The answer is yes, as it should be. In the US, the government actually works for the people; or they are supposed to. That's what elections are all about. We vote for the people who will represent us. The government was set up as a Republic form of government. Should the people be able to threaten the government? No, that would violate laws that forbid us from making threats on anyone's life. That's an *assault*, which can include a threat to someone's personal safety.

Does Mateen have the right to hate the US Government, Christians, Club Pulse, or alternative lifestyles? Yes, he does. However, he does not have the right to kill them.

The fact is, there are thousands, and perhaps millions of budding "Mateens" out there, hating everything Mateen hated. Is that a crime? No.

Changing the First Amendment to prevent this crime will not work. If the Amendment goes away, the haters will just be less vocal about it. It doesn't mean they won't act by carrying out more hate crimes. Remember, criminals don't obey the law.

Is the Second Amendment the Problem?

What about the Second Amendment? Should the people have the right to bear arms? This US amendment states, "A well-regulated militia being necessary to the security of a free State, the right of the people to keep and bear arms shall not be infringed."

As politicians banter back and forth, this seems to be the hottest issue. "Gun Control" sounds logical: take away guns, and you won't have shooters.

Would Mateen have been stopped if it were illegal for him to possess a weapon such as a gun? This may be a sticky issue for you, but the truth is, it would not have stopped him. This is a false security mindset.

Go into any prison system and the guards can produce boxes of weapons taken from prisoners, guns included. I've seen a box just like this presented at my local police department. Even in the small town we live in, these weapons exist.

Few criminals buy their guns at the local gun store. Mateen did, because he didn't care if the gun traced back to him. He probably expected to give his life for his cause. It would have been easy to buy the gun on the black market. Like drugs and prostitution, every town is well equipped. But even if he had not had the guns, he could have made explosives out of legal fertilizers.

Gun control advocates are simply living in column-one, protection. The fact is, the Second Amendment is equipping the general public with the understanding that law enforcement can't protect the individual. It also provides a level of protection against a tyrannical government takeover; something our Founding Fathers understood as they fled their mother country.

Think again about your own home security system. If the alarm goes off, detection has done its job. Response is next. If your response plan takes 20 minutes to execute, you're no better off than Club Pulse. Remember, the shooting spree will only last for eleven minutes, or maybe less if it's just you and your spouse. What's your plan?

If guns were illegal, Mateen would have simply developed a new plan, or acquired his gun on the streets. Remember, only law-abiding citizens obey the law.

Is the Club at Fault?

There are no easy answers. Could the club have predicted this mass shooting? Probably not, but the impact vs. likelihood graph is a measurement every club, (or no-gun zone), should be considering. All no-gun zones are *soft targets*.

However, the protection of the club has to be the responsibility of that club. If it takes the police that long to respond, just like a bank, jewelry store, or airline, the company might need more than bouncers with big muscles to stop an attack. It's a simple, non-optional principle of security. There has to be *detection and real-time response*.

How did Mateen get into the club with an assault rifle and a handgun in the first place? There was obviously inadequate detection/response at the door. Had this been in South Africa, you can be sure he would have had to walk through a metal detector before entering. The men at the door would have been armed. Mateen might have pulled out his guns at that point, and one or two of the doormen would have been taken out. But others nearby would have been ready to take him down. Worst case, there would have been two deaths: one bouncer, and Mateen.

But with the club not having encountered this type of event in the past, they were not paying bouncers to train with and carry weapons. The question is, in the future will the, arm their team to respond? Remember, detection is only as good as the timed response plan.

The Traditional Mindset: No One Will Break In

If you think you can stop the perpetrator, or that your firm is an unlikely target, you're probably wrong. It's the traditional mindset that, "We're safe, and no one will hurt us."

In the physical world, there are certain industries, people groups, and areas of the city that present high risk. But remember, when connecting to the Internet, you are directly connecting to the most committed criminals in the world. The traditional mindset says:

- ☐ It could never happen here. We have people watching our logs.

- ☐ It could never happen here because our data is not really worth anything. Besides, our company is too small and we live in the middle of nowhere.

- ☐ If we see something malicious, we'll figure out what to do. It's too expensive to worry about it right now.

- ☐ Risk isn't really measureable.

- ☐ If I don't see anything, it must mean everything is okay.

- ☐ It's in our budget for next year. We should be okay until that time.

☐ Security is too expensive. There's no return on investment.

The "Poised to Respond" Mindset Defined: Expect that People Are Trying to Break in. Don't Be Surprised to Find People Are Already in. Be Ready to Respond With Force

Hackers are sending out malware every day to gain access to any and all networks. Botnets are large systems of infected computers, taken over by hackers and their control servers. Every computer is a possible addition. About 250,000 computers are added to these botnets every day.

The attack often takes time. But undetected, you won't know about it until it actually happens to you. Computer time is measured in nanoseconds or faster. The faster computers get, the faster hacks will take place. Your team needs to understand that, like the police department, you can't detect and manually stop an attack like ransomware.

It also takes skill. Had Club Pulse armed their bouncers, it's possible that they could have taken down the perpetrator. However, with some training, the likelihood increases. A little known fact is that police officers are required to qualify for shooting only once or twice each year. Many of them are less qualified marksmen than you would think. But most criminals are even worse. They only shoot when in a gun fight, and that means, in a first offense, they may have zero training. In almost every case, they have had little or no training.

In the computer world, things are different. Computer criminals are working every day to build more sophisticated attacks and to avoid detection. They are well practiced, and prepared for the attack. The untrained security professional will be no match for these computer-savvy thieves.

☐ The "Trade Craft" of computer security response requires that you have individuals who understand what an attack looks like, and who know what to do once one is detected.

☐ Those responsible for creating and using data should be trained to know what misuse looks like, and to expect that it will happen. There should be a clear and easy process for users to report anything that looks suspicious.

☐ Those charged with actually watching over the detection side of security should be well prepared, with an escalation path and knowledge of forensics and chain of custody, to properly secure computers and report breaches.

☐ Like a disaster recovery plan, response teams need practice more than once each year. Companies on the alert often set up red and blue teams. Red teams are charged with simulating attacks that are then responded to by the blue teams.

☐ If your company is too small to have the right level of expertise on staff (and many are), you should immediately set up a managed security program through an experienced third party Security Operations Center (SOC). Just saying that they "do security" is not enough.

Adopting the Right Mindset: People Are Getting in. Your Mission: Find Them and Stop Them

Pen-testing Should Fail Every Time!

The idea of pen-testing, (or penetration testing), is to see if the systems are secure. The problem with this approach is that a true pen test should use the same techniques a hacker would use to gain access. That means social engineering is central to the pen-testing effort.

There's no point in testing all kinds of esoteric attack tools. Instead, simply hire some woman to friend your co-workers on

Facebook. Like the woman mentioned earlier, nine times out of ten, she'll get in. Note: the old trick of putting USB drives in the parking lot still works, but let's be a little more creative.

- ☐ Pen-testing should use the most likely methods to break in, not the coolest. In most cases, social engineering, or the ability to talk someone into giving up a password, is far more powerful than trying to hack through a firewall.

- ☐ Social Engineers target non-technical people who are too busy to check into who's asking and why they need something. In the end, if the office worker is a team player, they'll give in, and the hacker will have access.

- ☐ Most companies use scanners to pen test. They are looking for openings in the security perimeter. Using social engineering, the hacker no longer needs an opening. The user will create one for them. Scanners are necessary, but in many cases, the amateur's only tool. More is needed to assess risk.

Assessments Should Reveal Problems

Working with security consulting groups, I understand that only about 15% of the security assessments being done actually turn into remediation projects. Yet, just about every security assessment turns up critical issues. Why is this true?

There's a disconnect.

Looking at the assessment reports being submitted, I think I know what it is. The security engineer doing the work sees the problems, but reports them using technical jargon. He's so used to seeing these issues, "Because they show up on every network," that he is numb to it all. It's not that big of a deal. He thinks that just by showing you his raw data, you'll take action.

It would be like an oncologist finding some cancer in every patient. He would be so used to seeing it that it would no longer shock him. He might become numb to the urgency. From there, he would deliver the bad news in a stoic manner, using Latin phrases from his medical text books. You don't really understand, so you don't do anything about it. There is no impact vs. likelihood picture, so you don't know what it all means.

He's not sure why, but to him it doesn't really matter. He's on to the next patient. Of course, that's not how it really goes. When an oncologist sees cancer, he confirms it, and then meets with that patient and their loved ones. He explains in simple English, and often gives a likelihood; (his prognosis). "You have an 80% chance of beating this if you follow the protocol."

- ☐ Assessments should measure business risk. They should be building the impact vs. likelihood graph. In most cases, there should be several "Highly Likely" problems.

- ☐ Problems should always be brought back to a business issue, giving management something they understand and a way to respond, a measure of risk. Many security consultants will tell you this is impossible to measure. If they do, find another firm to assess your risk.

- ☐ If your assessments don't show problems, you might want to hire an new assessment team as well. Hackers are always one step ahead, meaning your risk is always changing.

Establish a Practice of Constant Interrogation

No one likes to be interrogated, but your computers need to be. Expecting attacks means constantly looking, thinking you must have missed something. If you live in the southeast, you sort of expect there to be cockroaches and termites. If you don't see any, you're probably not looking in the right place.

Once you see termite damage, it's too late. By the time it shows up, your house will be falling down. So instead, you hire a pest control company to investigate on a quarterly basis. Usually, in the southeast, they find colonies of termites underground. The goal is to keep them from coming into the wood.

Cockroaches aren't as harmful to your home, but they do carry all kinds of filthy diseases. The problem is, once you see one, you know there are millions of them hiding nearby. They don't usually come out until the lights are off. If you do see one, it's generally because you caught it by surprise while getting a midnight snack.

In both cases, if you live in the southeast, you just assume they are there and take preventative measures. Constant interrogation means:

- ☐ Assessments are continuous, or at least frequent (Quarterly would be a minimum requirement).

- ☐ Data is being watched continuously, knowing people are trying to get in.

- ☐ Highly sensitive areas of your company are constantly monitored with the understanding that, where there is secrecy and high-valued data, there is temptation, (accounting comes to mind).

End-User Response Requires End-User Training

Real-time response requires that you get your team involved. Like law enforcement, your security team can't see everything all the time. It's helpful to have everyone onboard. Those who create and use data should be trained to spot security issues, know what invites hackers, and understand what to do about it.

This can't be like the bouncers at Club Pulse. If your team doesn't know what to do when something looks suspicious, they won't do anything. Instead, create a clear path of escalation, ongoing training, and a culture that invites them to report strange activities without compromising their co-worker relationships or being made to feel like a whistleblower.

Before my family attended the Citizen's Police Academy, we really didn't understand what to report and when to call 911. Of course if we witnessed an accident, or thought someone was breaking in, we would make the call.

Our local police chief encouraged us to be watching and reporting strange activities. One afternoon, my oldest daughter took our son down to the park. While there, a man who appeared to be intoxicated arrived with a little girl. The girl's clothes were tattered and blood stained, and she was bruised. However, she didn't appear to be in distress.

A few weeks ago, my daughter would have wondered about it. But in this case she made the call. We don't know what became of the situation, but now, having been told to report this type of thing, we at least believe it was checked out. My daughter remains anonymous, and perhaps the girl has been rescued from something tragic. Perhaps the man will get some much needed help.

☐ End-users need to join forces with security. Since they create the data, and use it, they are the closest to it.

☐ As end-users better understand how security works, they'll become more serious about how they handle data. Knowing how hackers work, and what social engineering looks like can go a long way in protecting your company.

☐ Once your end-users really know what to look for, and what to do about it, they will be a welcome extension of your security team.

New Innovations Lead to Unexpected Problems

Digitalization is here. In the next ten years, expect major disruptions in business as technology evolves. This is not a bad thing. It's the next industrial revolution.

Back in the first industrial revolution, we didn't see men trying to work faster than an assembly line. Instead, they embraced it as a way to produce more, faster. Technology in the future means self-driving cars, more crowd-source companies like Airbnb and Uber, deep machine learning, and more forms of digital money. It means being connected to customers in new ways, and providing your customers with better solutions that build greater loyalty and longevity.

Jobs will disappear, new jobs will open up, and data will become more valuable as computers become more intelligent.

But with all of this comes a change in security. The more data you aggregate, the more it's worth, and the more you care about data security. With more data, you'll know much more about your customers, your marketing strategies, your competition, and where to take your company for greater profitability.

With technology changes come new vulnerabilities. Remember, all software has bugs, so when you add software, you add open doors. New software is more social. That means you're connecting more to the outside world. In order to do that, you are opening up new doors, and potentially eliminating that thing we used to call, "perimeter security." Some things to think about...

☐ New types of technology require new types of assessments and new approaches to security.

☐ Being outside the firewall, and working on phones, tablets, and in coffee shops, means working on the same network that your enemies are on. The bigger the network, the more likely you'll be attacked. If it's a citywide network, you can bet there are many hackers sharing that same network, watching you.

☐ More connected inevitably means more vulnerable. Equip your team with the understanding that people really do want your data. Assume they are trying to get it, and question every invitation, every email, every link, etc., before moving forward.

ACTION ITEMS TO ENABLE YOUR BUSINESS WITH SECURITY

✓ Get everyone one on board. Your data is of high value no matter how big your company is. People want it, and they'll work to get it.

✓ Contract with experts, or build your own. Either way, you need a team that possesses the trade craft to detect and stop threats.

✓ Constantly assess, and don't take "Okay" for an answer. There are problems to address and changes to make as you adopt new technology.

✓ Constantly train your people to be vigilant and to be an extension of your security team. They should know what breaches look like, what misuse looks like internally, what social engineering looks like, and what to do about it. In the end, they must be willing to take action.

Getting Your Company Focused on Security Enablement

☐ Remember, people are trying to get in. Hackers don't need to know your company domain or even its name to attack you. Spam is sent out to massive lists, and we are all on them.

☐ Talk about security internally. Make sure people understand how companies are breached and why. The more they know, the more likely they'll be to spot problems.

☐ End-users that don't know can't keep themselves from opening doors for hackers.

CHAPTER NINETEEN

Putting it All Together

Protection, detection, response…the problem with data security has a lot to do with wrong mindsets. Thinking security is someone else's responsibility, and that, if they do their job your data will be safe, is simply wrong thinking. All of us are in a war. And if we don't change our mindsets, we will lose our data.

Is your data secure? In most cases, you won't have seen much, (if any), in the way of direct security breaches on your network. But the truth is, most companies have had bots on their computers, (Over 90%), and every major company has, according to the Wall Street Journal, been compromised at some point.

To believe otherwise is to risk everything you've worked for up to this point. The hacker's tools are powerful. Social engineering always gets in, and more technology and automation is opening new doors every day. You can't stop hackers. You can only get better at detecting data theft, and stopping it before it's too late.

How to Get Started With Effective Security

I've touched on the big trends. Over time, you'll hear about new threats, but in most cases they'll leverage the seven trends I covered in Part-I. Malware will morph and increase in power, while social engineering will likely continue to be central to most large scale attacks. As Nation-States increase their attacks, (and they will), they'll use these tools just like every other hacker.

The important thing here is to understand who is actively attacking, what they want, and how they are doing it. Trends come and go. One year hacktivism will be big, while the next will be terrorism. If you know what the primary actors are up to, you will know what to be watching for when it comes to malware and social engineering ruses.

Your First Priority is Impact vs. Likelihood

Without an accurate measure of risk, you have no real guidelines for securing your business. With an understanding of your data and the possible impact, a measure of likelihood is your first step toward securing digital assets.

If your business has primarily relied on column one, (Protection), there's a high likelihood that you have malware on some of your systems. Going back to Part-I, malware is often the tool installed by unauthorized users from the outside, to gain entry. Once installed, they have access to your data, your computer, and anything they can use or learn from you through your computer. In this case, your likelihood is 100%. It's already happened. This is a normal, first finding for any company who has not already moved to a detection/response security model. If you have not done this type of assessment, now is the time.

Whether you find malware or not, there are probably other issues that will produce a high likelihood of compromise. Expect to find that some of your key applications show 80-90% likelihood ratings. If you look at some of the annual security breach reports, you'll see that many companies report a high rate of security incidents over the course of a year, regardless of how much they are spending on security.

Getting Real Measurements

In this book, I am recommending that you get an accurate, quantitative risk number. Don't let service providers and security consultants tell you it can't be done. Again, I'll refer you to the book, *How to Measure Anything*, by Douglas Hubbard. Measurement strategies are beyond the scope of this book, but Hubbard will give you important insights which I personally used in my own quantitative risk analysis work earlier in my career.

The problem is, many consultants have not taken the time to understand measurements, and have been too lazy to develop a system of measuring risk. If health professionals can do it, security consultants can too.

These measurements should be applied to the various applications in your business based on where they sit, who uses them, the type of data they house, (think data value), and the climate of your business right now.

These assessments are a snapshot in time. That means they will need to be updated on a quarterly basis. The more you know, the better your decisions will be. As Hubbard points out, before you measure, you should know what those measurements are leading to and what questions you are trying to answer. The question, "Are we secure?" is not a valid question. Rather, you should be asking, "What are the chances we will be compromised, (or some other security issue will occur), in the next 12 – 18 months, and where will it most likely happen?"

In other words, if there is a 90% chance that your disk will fail, will you replace it? If there's a 77% chance that your backups won't restore properly in the event of a disk failure, will you correct the problem? What steps would bring that percentage into a reasonable range?

There's no point in measuring unless you first know what it is you're aiming to do based on the findings.

Fixing the One Big Issue

The big issue should now be clear. We were told to keep hackers out. In theory, that's right. However, understanding that the hacker is always one step ahead, helps us by pointing us in a new direction. Like physical break-ins, you can't really keep people out. So a move to detection, with a real-time response is necessary. How do you do that?

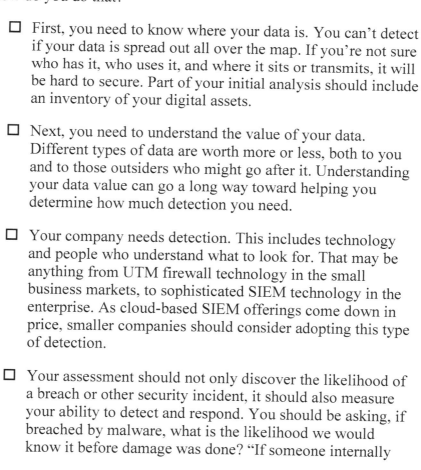

- ☐ First, you need to know where your data is. You can't detect if your data is spread out all over the map. If you're not sure who has it, who uses it, and where it sits or transmits, it will be hard to secure. Part of your initial analysis should include an inventory of your digital assets.

- ☐ Next, you need to understand the value of your data. Different types of data are worth more or less, both to you and to those outsiders who might go after it. Understanding your data value can go a long way toward helping you determine how much detection you need.

- ☐ Your company needs detection. This includes technology and people who understand what to look for. That may be anything from UTM firewall technology in the small business markets, to sophisticated SIEM technology in the enterprise. As cloud-based SIEM offerings come down in price, smaller companies should consider adopting this type of detection.

- ☐ Your assessment should not only discover the likelihood of a breach or other security incident, it should also measure your ability to detect and respond. You should be asking, if breached by malware, what is the likelihood we would know it before damage was done? "If someone internally were stealing money from us, what is the likelihood we would discover it before the cost exceeded X?"

☐ Does the response system work? If you know you can detect, (E.g. your home alarm system), do you have an adequate response plan that follows?

☐ Once your assessment is in place, you'll want to develop a security plan; a road map that will guide you from your current state, to a future, more desirable state.

☐ With your plan in motion, a team of people is necessary to watch for alerts. People often ask me if computers or robots be able to do the alert analysis now or at some point in the future. At this time, I don't recommend it. At some point, this type of analysis will be more feasible. Advancements in deep learning computers and big data analytics certainly make this a future goal. But for now, invest in the right people. For mid-market and smaller firms, this is likely an outsourced program. Seek out qualified, security focused IT management companies.

☐ Finally, your people are the first line of defense. Make sure they know what they are looking for, and what to do when something doesn't look right.

Where to Go Next

Once you have measurements in place, and you've discovered how well equipped you are to detect and respond, you're ready to start working on your organization. Remember, your people are part of your security team, building a culture that understands and supports data security. This is a necessary step in today's digitalized business environment.

Re-engineering the Mindsets/ Transforming the People

Bruce Schneier, in his book *Secrets and Lies*, identifies *people* as your biggest problem. Looking across your company, each person must understand their role, their access privileges, and the value of the data they create, touch, or have rights to. They should also have some understanding of why they don't have rights to other data. There are many roles and many access levels, as well as responsibilities across the organization. Let's consider a few.

Board Members

☐ Lawsuits are being filed regularly against boards, alleging misconduct. Data compromise affects partners, suppliers, and customers. You can expect these lawsuits to grow if board members continue to delegate the overall responsibility of security, without understanding impact vs. likelihood.

☐ Board meetings should incorporate a security review. A typical, two-day board meeting might include at least 30 minutes of security discussion to explore the company's current state and exposure. The impact vs. likelihood graph should be central to this discussion.

☐ An oversight committee should be established to better understand security policies, standards, and procedures. Security policies are often neglected, but are the key to limiting liability and driving network and system architecture.

☐ Retain security advisors. This is especially true for midsized and small businesses. Since full-time security expertise is expensive, it is imperative that business leaders have someone knowledgeable to call on when making strategic decisions that include technology and data. Consider someone in a virtual CISO if your organization is too small to support a full-time, qualified person in this role.

CEO's & Presidents – Get Involved

Executives and business owners are what I call *Asset Owners*. An asset owner is really anyone who has liability when it comes to data. If your home were to catch fire, even though you probably have homeowner's insurance, it would be costly. You might even suffer the loss of a family member. That's liability.

Four things every business leader needs to know:

- ✓ What constitutes your most important digital assets, and where they are at any given time.
- ✓ Your top 3 to 5 most pressing threats.
- ✓ The odds that you'll suffer impact against one of your identified digital assets or applications (over the next 12 months).
- ✓ How your company security is trending. Is it getting better or worse?

In addition, there are security responsibilities that come with business leadership: governance, policy, procedures, people, and more. Consider the following:

- ☐ IT departments require oversight. Speaking as a former IT director, working for one of the largest banks in the US, I can say with confidence that IT rarely understands the value of data, or the changing business climates that affect risk levels. The C-suite must ensure this is happening.

- ☐ Require a written security plan. Policies govern aspects of security such as usage and architectural standards. A plan should be put in place to create a roadmap from the organization's current state to the proposed future. Company leaders should be intimately involved in this process.

☐ Maintain insurance. Cyberinsurance is often necessary to cover things that are not covered by your company's corporate insurance and general liability policies. Regular audits should be conducted and overseen by the board to determine the extent to which the company is (or can be) insured against a data breach.

☐ Security leadership should have functional ties into all organizations that affect governance for the organization. The CISO should have influence and a level of control over any and all security related procedures and strategies within the organization.

☐ The CISO is a position of power within the organization. This level of responsibility should not be given to anyone other than an executive who understands data security and risk exposure. Too many smaller businesses have given the CISO title to individuals who lack the experience and level of liability to carry out this role. Ultimately, the CISO should have the authority to examine all data and access across the enterprise, to better evaluate the protection levels over any given asset.

☐ Require regular risk assessments. These assessments should uncover major threats and vulnerabilities, and provide a measurement of likelihood that is understandable to board level members. It is imperative that the leadership team be involved in this process.

☐ Ultimately, the CISO is responsible for people and their activities. Remember, security is more of a people problem than it is a technical one. A person's role within the company often determines what kinds of data they handle, what they create, and how they carry out their work with regard to corporate data. Any large-scale personnel change is likely to have a great impact on the company's security posture.

☐ In the event of an incident, it is the CISO who is responsible for overseeing the response.

Note: While I have related all of these responsibilities to the CISO, a company that only has a CIO or a small business owner, operating without a dedicated IT function, would then take on the responsibilities of the CISO described above.

IT Personnel

Today, there is a shortage of qualified, talented people who understand data science, security, and transformational technologies. At the same time, there is a growing need for greater expertise on how to identify risk, understand data value, and detect misuse or an outright attack before damage is done.

The role of IT, with regard to security, is simply to implement and maintain the systems that PROTECT, DETECT, and RESPOND to an incident.

It's a custodial function; one of technology oversight, protection of data, and the maintenance of systems. It is not a position of liability. Therefore, it is incumbent on corporate leadership to require and understand risk reports and recommendations that come from IT, and to take seriously any reports of possible misuse or attacks. Like in a war, it is the general who is responsible for planning and approving major operations, not the actual platoon.

The following considerations should be understood:

☐ Larger companies should maintain a dedicated security team.

☐ Security is a tradecraft. It requires constant fine tuning and participation to stay on top. If your company is not large enough to employ a dedicated team, it may be time to outsource this function. It is almost impossible to maintain security experts in midsize companies since there are not enough security issues to keep a dedicated team interested or well-trained.

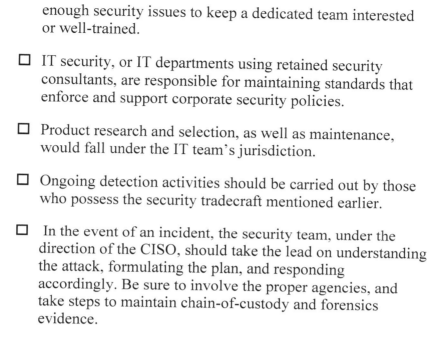

☐ IT security, or IT departments using retained security consultants, are responsible for maintaining standards that enforce and support corporate security policies.

☐ Product research and selection, as well as maintenance, would fall under the IT team's jurisdiction.

☐ Ongoing detection activities should be carried out by those who possess the security tradecraft mentioned earlier.

☐ In the event of an incident, the security team, under the direction of the CISO, should take the lead on understanding the attack, formulating the plan, and responding accordingly. Be sure to involve the proper agencies, and take steps to maintain chain-of-custody and forensics evidence.

Re-engineering the Mindset of The End-User

End-users, or knowledge workers, have largely been left out of the security equation. Newer compliance regulations dictate the need for security awareness training, but few companies take this seriously. Security training is often considered an extra expense, time consuming, and not very interesting. Anything you can do to make this process more interesting will pay off in the long run.

The end-user has been called by some, the "New Firewall." Historically, users sat behind the firewall, working on terminals and PCs at their desk. Today's workers are online all day, on the phone, using tablets, working in coffee shops, and traveling around the world.

What the end-user does as they create, use, and delete data, greatly affects the overall security of the organization. Remember, your weakest link defines your company's security strength. End-users must…

☐ Understand the value of their own data in terms of dollars.

☐ Have a basic knowledge of who is out there stealing data, why they steal, and how they steal.

☐ Be able to detect a problem, know what to do about it, and be willing to take action.

☐ Understand best practices and the policies that dictate data access, creation, transmission, usage, and deletion.

☐ Be involved in ongoing security awareness training programs. End-users are the easiest targets for social engineering experts. The better you can equip your team to spot a ruse quickly, the more secure your company will be.

Partners and Third-Party Suppliers

Another area often neglected is that of vendors and partners. Automation, digitalization, and the need for connectedness are introducing all kinds of new risks to businesses. In a recent security assessment, we found a small bank using a third-party check processing service. The connection between them was direct. Connections like this are common, but are a major flaw in a firm's security architecture. In this case it could have cost the bank millions if it had been detected by the wrong people.

Some things to consider:

☐ The weak link defines your overall security. You have the right and responsibility to review the security posture of any and all connected partners.

☐ Require some level of security assessment before giving partners access to your systems. If possible, access should be granted through a DMZ, not directly to your production systems.

☐ Limit access. Like you do with internal employees, access should be given on a need-to-know basis. In this case, you may have little recourse if something goes wrong. This is especially true if your partner is overseas, such as a contracted programmer from India or the Ukraine.

Classify Your Data, Create Your Policies, and Educate Your People

Moving forward, your organization needs to know where the data is, what's important, and how to deal with it. There are many books written on security policies, but in a nutshell, you need policies, procedures, standards, and guidelines.

Policies

Policies do two things: drive architecture and limit liability. They don't actually protect anything. SANS, *www.sans.org*, offers a free set of generic policies that can be modified. For the small business, this is a good place to start. For larger organizations, I would recommend bringing in a consultant that specializes in building security policies.

In order for your policies to work for you, they must be well defined and enforceable. Unenforced policies are often seen as recommendations if your company is ever involved in a lawsuit surrounding a security breach. You'll need to show that your policies are up-to-date and have been read and understood by all employees. If someone can produce a policy that has been violated with some frequency without repercussion, the court will likely rule all of your policies in that area as recommendations.

The other point I will make is that your *policies* should be fairly generic. Use *procedures* and *standards* to name specifics. For instance, the policy might state that you need a password for a system. The standard would call for a specific recipe. By doing this, you will ease the burden of maintaining up-to-date policies. It is also helpful to maintain a set of very short, to-the-point policies, rather than one mammoth document. So a set of policies would include individual policies such as, "Remote Access Policy," "Data Access Policy," etc. By doing this, it is easy to add a new policy such as your BYOD policy.

Procedures

Procedures are lists of things to be carried out. They are the "how." So if your policy says that everyone must have a password, it is then issued by a procedure and in accordance with a standard. The standard calls for eight characters, using an alphanumeric sequence. The procedure shows how a password is issued, and how it is revoked, (such as upon employee exit).

Standards

The standards will change more than anything. You might specify brands, or just types of technology to be used. For instance, you might have a policy stating that you will encrypt all remote access traffic. The standard might call for AES, which is in itself a standard that points to an encryption algorithm. The industry maintains the algorithm by which the current AES encryption standard is satisfied. All you need to know is that your company is following the current AES standard, (which is part of the NIST framework), so you won't have to change your standard even if the industry comes up with a new AES standard algorithm. If AES and NIST are new to you, they're probably not important to your role in the company. They are detailed and complex security terms that may require further study for those responsible for actually setting the standards used by your company.

Guidelines

Finally, the guidelines are recommendations. This is a great place to add things that you recommend, but are not enforceable. You might require each person to have a standard password, set by a procedure. A guideline might encourage some best practices while traveling or working at home.

Establish a Road Map to Remediation

Once your assessment is done, with a completed impact vs. likelihood graph, your organization should establish a roadmap. It's your plan to get from where you are to where you are going. It's your remediation plan.

Urgent issues should be addressed immediately. But there will be other recommendations that should be carried out over time. For instance, all companies do need a policy; however, policy is rarely urgent. Your compliance officer may be pushing for a policy to be written, but in most cases it will be on the roadmap for completion during the next quarter.

When an assessment is completed, it seems like little attention is given to the recommendations. This may be due to the esoteric nature of the recommendations being made. Insist that your assessment team be specific about what does need to be done, and then get clarification on what they are recommending. Your assessment initiative should lead to a punch list, or a roadmap of specific actions your company is going to take over some period of time.

Without this type of documented plan, you may find that your company never actually makes the recommended changes. When another security incident occurs, you can expect a lot of finger pointing. Be proactive; strike anything that isn't necessary, and create a plan to execute on those things that are truly justified.

Finally, your goal is to have a balanced security architecture. One that offers a level of protection based on the value of your digital assets. Due-care, a term often used by security compliance officers, means adequate protection given the data you create, use, and transmit in your organization. This is what your company would need to show if there were a lawsuit brought on by a breach.

☐ Make the shift. Compliance is not security. However, you do need to meet your industry's compliance requirements.

☐ Stop thinking about firewalls and passwords. These are all necessary things. However, your focus should be on assets and your organization's impact vs. likelihood graph.

☐ Continue to improve your level of security intelligence. Make incremental changes, looking for the greatest returns based on measureable intelligence you receive from your security management team. Remember, everything is measureable, including risk.

☐ Test your response program regularly. In the physical world, detection is often pretty good. The weak link is response. As you and your team work to improve detection, remember that response follows closely in importance.

Spread the Word; Become the Next Security Evangelist

Compliance requirements are fast becoming one of your company's most unproductive budget line items. The more hackers succeed, the more government will respond with additional compliance laws. Keep in mind that these law-creators are often lacking in real-world security expertise. Worse, the laws are made by committee, not consensus. At the end of the day, you can believe that 5 people had 5 different opinions, and somehow the next new requirement was not at the top of any one person's list. It's just all they could agree to at that moment.

The more you can encourage your peers and colleagues to take steps toward the things in this book, and those recommended by top security consultants around the world, the more secure companies will become. And without great losses being reported, the expansion of government oversight will hopefully slow.

Make wise use of your security budget, and point others to the same. In the end it will save us all time and money, and allow us all to get back to the business activities we really care about.

ABOUT DAVID STELZL

David Stelzl, CISSP brings a fresh perspective on the security of your digital assets, which are fast becoming your digital money. His analogies are simple to understand, allowing business leaders to get involved in keeping their company's most important and most valuable secrets safeguarded.

He has authored several books including *Data@Risk*, *The House & The Cloud*, and *From Vendor to Advisor*, and has worked with technology companies around the world to show them how to measure risk, how to make risk understandable to business leaders, and how to help organizations build a secure mindset as they move into the Digitalization Megatrend.

Stelzl Visionary Learning Concepts, Inc. has consulted with, addressed, and been sponsored by industry leading companies such as Cisco Systems, Hewlett Packard, Ingram Micro, Trend Micro, Symantec, Check Point, Juniper, Kaspersky, and many associations and businesses in the financial, pharmaceutical, and high-tech markets.

David earned his CISSP certification in 2000, and has worked in the information security business since 1995.

71690250R00122

Made in the USA
San Bernardino, CA
17 March 2018